Evolution

and the

Nature of

Good

Douglas H

Shennan

Order this book online at www.trafford.com
or email orders@trafford.com

Most Trafford titles are also available at major online book retailers.

© Copyright 2009 Douglas Shennan.
Cover design by Kenneth M Green, 6a Th e Grove, Leisure Isle, Knysna
6570, South Africa.
Telephone (0027) 44 384 1895.

Note for Librarians: A cataloguing record for this book is available from Library
and Archives Canada at www.collectionscanada.ca/amicus/index-e.html

Printed in Victoria, BC, Canada.

ISBN: 978-1-4269-0193-5 (soft)
ISBN: 978-1-4269-0229-1 (hard)
ISBN: 978-1-4269-0253-6 (ebook)

*Our mission is to efficiently provide the world's finest, most comprehensive
book publishing service, enabling every author to experience success.
To find out how to publish your book, your way, and have it available
worldwide, visit us online at www.trafford.com*

Trafford rev. 10/6/2009

TraFForD PUBLISHING® www.trafford.com

North America & international
toll-free: 1 888 232 4444 (USA & Canada)
phone: 250 383 6864 ♦ fax: 812 355 4082

PREFACE

This is the third and last of my offerings on the significance of human evolution for modern people. The first, *Evolution and the Spiral of Technology*, describes the way the evolutionary pressures on our ancestors led our line to develop an ever-changing culture and an unsustainable way of life. The second, *Evolution and the Nature of Reality*, points to the limits to our knowledge imposed by the way we have evolved.

The fact that hominid and human society was more stable before it was overtaken by the rat-race gives an indication of how we should *behave*, and this book is about that. Like its predecessors, it largely uses secondary sources whose authors, themselves experts, have already digested original writers and drawn informed conclusions. Many disciplines are involved, and I make no claim to be expert at any of them. The claim inherent in these books, however, is to have discovered a cross-disciplinary approach that opens up a more panoramic view of the world and a more comprehensive understanding of human affairs.

My thanks go to Anne-Marie Chappell and Liz Sharp, both of whom reviewed the draft and made many useful comments, as a result of which not only detail but also the method of presentation was altered.

GLOSSARY

Some words are used here in a particular sense that may not be obvious to all readers. With apologies to those who are familiar with them, the following list is offered.

Apes	Animals descended from monkeys, without tails and having the greatest intellectual development among non-human animals. Modern apes include chimpanzees, gorillas, orang-utans and gibbons, and have a common ancestor with hominids and humans.
Charity	A non-critical acceptance of other people and their behaviour, together with a willingness to co-operate with them and help them. It differs from kindness in that it involves an attitude as well as action.
Cro-Magnon	The earliest form of modern human found in Europe, where remains found date back to about 35,000 years ago.
Culture	The ability of individuals to pass on information about their experience to others, including children. It enables species to make rapid adaptations to their environment, instead of relying on the slow process of natural selection.

Dogma	A tenet which is maintained through faith, and which is therefore not amenable to change by argument.
Faith	Belief which is regarded as of primary importance, and is not abandoned because of evidence presented.
Hominids	Several species descended from early apes, and from one of which humans are in turn descended. They are sometimes referred to as "the missing link".
Hunter-gatherers	Modern humans who lived off the land before the invention of farming, which was first practised about 12,000 years ago.
Natural selection	The process by which individuals less suited to their environment are either killed off or prevented from reproducing, and so cannot pass on their genes to offspring. It maintains the fitness of the species.
Neanderthal	An earlier form of human who survived in Europe until Cro-Magnon times but then became extinct. Modern people are not descended from them.

Objective	Describes observations which are made from outside the system being observed; for instance a psychiatrist may watch how a child reacts to toys and pictures.
Rational	Based on reason.
Reason	The intellectual faculty by which conclusions are drawn from premises. Essentially it is the antithesis of faith, in which a fixed belief is accepted and is not negotiable by argument. Reason differs from reductionism in that it can draw conclusions from subjective experience.
Reductionism	The analysis of complex things into simple constituents; the method used by scientists and mathematicians to draw conclusions from observations. It does not deal with subjective experience.
Reductive	Adjective of reductionism.
Species	A group of individuals genetically related closely enough to reproduce with each other.

Subjective   Describes observations made
                                        when the observer is part of the
                                        system being observed, such as
                                        being hungry, admiring a
                                        sunset, or saying "How awful!"

EVOLUTION AND THE NATURE OF GOOD
CONTENTS

Introduction

To do good unto others—to do unto others as ye would that
they do unto you—is the foundation-stone of morality.
Charles Darwin[1]

When the ancient Greeks started exploring the nature of the world
beneath its obvious features—the events that occur in it and the
functioning of people and animals in it—their primary concern was
with proper behaviour. That is what exercised Socrates, who was
himself a very moral man, and was willing to give his life rather
than compromise his principles. For Plato, his pupil and admirer,
Good is the source of light which reveals to us things as they really
are; Good is transcendent.[2] The concept of *truth*, as opposed to
right or good, followed soon afterwards. The idea of truth was
necessary in order to handle the complex ideas that the ancients had
now begun to deal with; instead of making an instinctive response,
the new thinkers would go through the process: observation,
conclusion (truth), decision, and finally action. In an earlier book,
Evolution and the Nature of Reality[3], I have discussed how, because
of the origins of humankind, the need for good (ethical behaviour,
mutual care, co-operation) is fundamental to the survival and
welfare of people, and the concept of truth is incidental. In other
words, for any particular species—including humans—good is
absolute, and is dictated by the need of its members to prosper and
survive. Truth, on the other hand, is not absolute but relative, and
differs for people in different situations. It is the product of

EVOLUTION AND THE NATURE OF GOOD

thought, and does not exist for animals that do not have a neo-cortex in the brain and so respond to situations instinctively. The "truth" of any situation is the assessment made of it by an individual as a preliminary to reacting to it.

In this way ethics was the mother of philosophy, not, as is usually assumed, the other way round.

It was natural that this should be the case. Insects and reptiles instinctively help other members of their own species; without such co-operation they could not survive. With the evolution of the mammalian brain, calculated co-operation has become part of the way of life of animals. The evolution of the brain has gone hand-in-hand with the development of culture. In this book the term "culture" is used in the biological sense, and means the ability to communicate ideas, especially to offspring, who can therefore benefit from the experience of their parents, enabling individuals to make rapid adjustments to their environment through learning in their lifetime, and not to be solely dependent on the slow adaptations handed down to them by natural selection.

Iris Murdoch stands out among modern philosophers in recognizing good as the fundamental reality for humans, although she does not relate this to our evolutionary past. She sees good as the only absolute: "Even the concept of Truth has its ambiguities and it is really only of Good that we can say 'it is the trial of itself and needs no other touch'."[4]

If Good is predominant, the question of whether we can choose what we do is important. In the earlier book mentioned I have put the case for the existence of free-will within a world which, seen from afar, is deterministic, governed by the laws of science and specifically, when it comes to ourselves, by the relentless process of

INTRODUCTION

evolution. The point is that, as discussed in that book, our view is in the first place subjective; it starts from birth within each one of us. We are introduced to the physical world later, and come to live in it and react to it. But from our subjective viewpoint, we can choose what we do; it does not matter that the global construct that we make of the physical world shows it to be deterministic.

What is right behaviour for humans depends entirely on our evolutionary history, our dependence on co-operation, and our species' inherited needs together with those additional needs resulting from our superimposed culture. Yet almost no writers on ethics show an awareness of biology or evolution. Even those who mention evolution often fail to grasp its central significance for ethical thought. In the words of Peter Singer, "To pursue questions about the origins and nature of ethics without looking at the full range of possible explanations is to remain wilfully ignorant. Yet, for most of this [20th] century, philosophers writing on ethics have focussed on what other philosophers writing on ethics have written. The discipline has become ingrown, scrutinizing narrowly framed questions that can be advanced by careful reasoning and argument, while ignoring whole bodies of knowledge about the nature of ethics that have accumulated in other fields of study."[5]

Some writers widen the scope of "ethics" to mean more than just what we *should* do. To some it is a description of how co-operative behaviour evolves, and to others it includes consideration of the needs of the decision-maker as well as of other people. Philippa Foot finds an objective, rational basis for morality by identifying ethics with proper biological functioning[6] and with expediency[7];

EVOLUTION AND THE NATURE OF GOOD

she embraces within morality good for oneself as well as for other people.

Moral behaviour, however, means doing things for the benefit of others (a broad term which can embrace not just humans but all living things) in preference to seeking immediate benefit to oneself. It has come about through the development of co-operation by individuals within all species, including humans. Reciprocity is found amongst all social mammals with long memories.[8]

Among modern Europeans and Americans there is much confusion about what *natural selection* means. Evolution by natural selection is a simple process. It depends on small random variations in individuals' genetic makeup, which may make them more suited or less suited to the physical environment in which the species lives, or less able to find food, or easier prey themselves. They are therefore more likely to die off, and over many generations this causes a change in the characteristics of the population. But "the survival of the fittest" has become a catch-phrase to excuse all kinds of competitive, predatory and discriminatory behaviour. Among the misconceptions that have arisen from a misunderstanding of natural selection are Herbert Spencer's thesis that the more materially successful people should be encouraged to breed and the less successful allowed to die off as far as possible, and the Nazi effort to purify the Aryan race by the slaughter of millions of people, which was a grotesque development of Spencer's idea. However, the same trend of thought finds its way into modern democratic society. To Adam Smith, the founder of economics, competition was the way to ensure prosperity and stability for the community; the object was to defeat others in trade rather than co-operate with them. Modern democracies have adopted this model, and the rule now is that the only people to be helped selflessly are one's own family and close friends.

But natural selection, that is the elimination of those individuals who are unfitted to their environment, applies as a simple process only to living things which have not developed an outer layer of grey matter, or neo-cortex, to the brain, a process that began with the evolution of our ancestors the early mammals about 200 million years ago. For those that have, and in this way have acquired the use of culture, mutual help and co-operation are indispensable features of their existence. Humans, far more than any other species, depend on it. Perversely, our culture has largely been used to oppose, fight against, and kill other humans, whereas other species do not destroy their own kind, but subjugate or temporarily disable them for sexual access, or for leadership and prestige. To survive and prosper we need to use our culture to maintain the co-operative mode of life that is natural to non-human animals. The Scottish philosopher David Hume recognized that people are naturally benevolent, even if towards a restricted circle, and that sympathy exists between them. These are reasons why people should behave ethically, though Hume believed they do not provide *proof* that they should. Hume's famous contention was that you cannot derive an "ought" from an "is", and, like his contemporaries, he saw moral behaviour as an "ought".[9] However, a recognition of the genetic origin of altruism, and its contribution towards human survival, stability and welfare, makes a rational derivation of moral behaviour possible.

Although this book is about good, I have expanded a little on truth because the very widely held misconception that truth is absolute and universal leads to gross injustice and cruelty. Those

EVOLUTION AND THE NATURE OF GOOD

who believe their truth to be important may lose their natural human instinct for kindness and co-operation, and apply sanctions and punishments to "convert" others. The archetype was the mediaeval and later persecution and burning at the stake of many heretics by the Church of Rome and the monarchs that supported it. However, far more widely and more recently people have been sidelined, disadvantaged and refused jobs because of their religious beliefs. The most sincere and well-disposed Christian fundamentalists will tell you that you will go to Hell for ever if you do not convert to their view of an anthropomorphic God before you die. A tangential question arises from this—how can one possibly choose what to believe? To each individual, action is chosen, but belief is inescapable.

Because good behaviour and mutual co-operation are so fundamental to modern human welfare and survival, our culture has developed in such a way as to encourage them. This has had to be done in a society that came very early on to believe in absolute truth. Ethical decisions, it was felt, could not be made without a set of truths to base them on. In this way the religions of the world have developed: God is, and God wishes you to behave in certain ways, which in general are beneficial to society as a whole. If you do not conform, God will punish you, either on this earth or hereafter.

Not only is God anthropomorphic, he is usually andromorphic; Jews, Christians and Muslims, for instance, have made God in the image of a human male. In this book I offer a God that is not anthropomorphic, but is no less real—indeed, it is easier to follow the dictates of this God because they are rationally derived and we can see *why* we are following them. My God is the spirit of

INTRODUCTION

goodness and mutual co-operation, passed down to us by our ancestors because it is essential to the survival of our species. My belief in this deity is based on science and deduction, and is as firm as that of the most ardent evangelist. It can be changed only if more information about human evolution indicates the need. For it seems clear to me that ethics is the reason for religion, and that the ethical course is to renounce the "I'm-all-right-Jack" western ideal of today, which has now penetrated to all parts of the world. In its place, I believe, we need to restore the spirit of co-operation and mutual help that much more closely characterises the non-human mammals, and, indeed, human hunter-gatherers—who had the immense advantage of living in groups of 50-100 people, thus achieving co-operation because all the members knew each other. The name of God derives from good with the elimination of one "o"—both come from a common Germanic root. God is about good, not about omnipotence or truth.

Views of what is right in contemporary ethical discussion vary between the extremes of, on the one hand, Kant's position, that one must do one's duty regardless of whether it is hurtful and damaging to oneself or even to others, and on the other hand, the simple market contract stance saying "We agree to behave in such a way because it will be to the advantage of both of us." But the way ethical behaviour has evolved since our cultural beginnings shows it to be supremely subjective: it is a tension between doing what is immediately satisfying for me as an individual and doing what will benefit others; in simple terms, it is about the resisting of temptation.

The advance of human culture means that our species has strayed far from a natural adjustment to the environment, which is

EVOLUTION AND THE NATURE OF GOOD

intrinsically and essentially ethical. We are constantly making changes and thinking of new technologies, which cause harm to other species, to the biosphere as a whole, to people of other races, and even to our fellows. We are so dependent on the changes we have brought about that we cannot undo them. Although the usual reaction expected when one acknowledges a fault is to repent and stop doing whatever it was, to think clearly about ethics it is necessary to accept that one is doing wrong things all the time and cannot reverse them, and to admit it. If we have to justify ourselves constantly we can never reach rational conclusions; to make sense of ethics one has to be a hypocrite.

Ethical behaviour is generally regarded as a human invention. Writers refer to humans as "the moral animal". But it follows from what has been said above that whereas pre-cultural species behave in an entirely moral fashion, humans had to create a concept and discipline of ethics precisely because their culture had led them to stray from normal co-operative moral conduct.

PART I
THE PHILOSOPHICAL BASIS OF ETHICS

Chapter 1
Goodness versus truth

Good is fundamental, truth incidental

The subjective origin of truth and knowledge

After I am born, the world begins to take shape round me. I see variations of light and shadow, and objects begin to form. The most important of these is my mother, who reacts to movements that I make. Life becomes a matter of relating to my mother. The first few months of my life are spent forming relationships with my mother and father and other people. Only later do I start to observe connections and interactions between objects in the world round me, and thereby conclude that there is a rational physical world.

EVOLUTION AND THE NATURE OF GOOD

In this way our life starts as a subjective phenomenon. And in its essential nature that is what it continues to be. The important thing to each of us throughout our lives is the relationships we form with other people. The physical world, the world of observation and reason and science, does appear in our lives some years after birth, but its sole purpose for each of us is to improve our adjustment to our environment, an essential element of which is our inter-personal relationships. This priority of the subjective over the objective, rational side of our lives is the subject of my earlier book *Evolution and the nature of reality*.[1]

The subjective element in ethics

Good is different to different people. If truth is different to each of us, as has been argued in the book mentioned, then likewise what is good is individually determined. Lenin's question "True for whom?" clearly also embraces "Good for whom?" The different nature, circumstances, and needs, not only of different species but of individuals within a species, mean that what is good for one is not necessarily good for the next. Solzhenitsyn pointed out that good and evil are different to different, often opposing, factions,[2] although A.C. Ewing has little sympathy with the idea that right and good can be different when assessed by different people.[3] According to the "subjective theory" of ethics, moral disagreement is merely a disagreement in attitude and not in belief;[4] it holds that subjectivism is fundamental in ethics, and that the reductive approach to determining proper behaviour is wrong because the internal point of view is centrally important.[5]

GOODNESS VERSUS TRUTH

Yet it can be argued that there is an absolute quality to good, and that it is biologically determined. The "emotive theory" holds that we use moral judgments, like exclamations, to vent emotions or to arouse emotions in other people.[6] The emotive view goes some way towards acknowledging that what is right is determined by our biological nature. Charity (tolerance), a quality which most would regard as good, is needed for socialization, but it is subjective; one exercises it to help other people, spontaneously, and does not calculate its results in terms of biological advantage. In any case we do not know enough about other people to work out what would be best for them. Our evolution guides us; charity is instinctive, even though its effects are in the interests of the species rather than the individual. As Portia tells Shylock in *The Merchant of Venice*:

> The quality of mercy is not strained;
> It droppeth as the gentle rain from heaven
> Upon the place beneath.

Human relations are the essence of reality to each of us

Thus the essence of reality for all humans stems from their relationship to living and non-living things, and not from the objective physical world. The *attitudes* that prevail between people are paramount. Such things are unknown to physics. Meaningful reality is not therefore to be discovered by reductionist means.

The only role of rationalism for humans is to derive relationships between themselves on the one hand, and living and non-living things outside themselves on the other. Although

EVOLUTION AND THE NATURE OF GOOD

the scientist sees this as adaptation to our environment, it is driven by our emotions and comes from within us.

The important thing for living things as a whole is how other living things and non-living objects will affect the being's adaptation. None of this involves a reductive process, and so it is not dealt with by using a rational approach.

Relationships depend on attitudes, not logic

We relate to everything in a two-sided way: the object is not independent of the observer (this indeed is a tenet of quantum theory). In relations with people this stance completely dominates our behaviour. Our attitude to them is not based on logical reasoning but on the relationship which exists between us. If we decide to be "rational", this requires an extra effort; we have to look at ourselves and them from the outside and analyse the situation reductively, like a problem in mathematics or engineering. This approach is used by biologists, behaviourists and sociobiologists.

Christianity and other religions teach us to respond without reasoning—to take an attitude which is uncritically charitable, to be prepared to seek the best in other people.

Our failure to do this is the cause of strife. In the successful computer strategy of "tit-for-tat", the best relationships are achieved by being generous the first time, and thereafter being selfish or generous, hostile or friendly, according to whether the other party has done the same. This strategy is, in the first instance at least, the same as that of the religions: our first move should be charitable and outgoing. The instinct for charity and reciprocity has been bred by natural selection to enable us to get more from social living.[7]   Other animals behave in the same way.

As an example, our daughter Elaine only has time for 3 days with us at Christmas because she has to mark examination papers. Her sister Jane invites her, through us, to California for Christmas.   There is no point in telling Elaine of Jane's invitation because she has no time. Why is this not true? It is the substitution of logic for the inter-relation between people; the latter reflects the reality. This is true whether Elaine would accept Jane's invitation or not. In the former case she might find it worth-while to re-arrange her work because of the goodwill Jane has shown in inviting her for a major holiday; in the latter case she has learned about her sister's goodwill.

The idea put forward of imposing rules on parents prohibiting smacking of children exemplifies well the influential public's misconception of the relations between people, in this case parents and children. It assumes a mechanistic and logical interaction between people, and ignores the fundamental importance of the attitudes they hold to one another. What is harmful is not smacking, but the wish to smack inappropriately, in response to irritation and intolerance of the child; it is not the decision, after cool thought, to correct the child's behaviour. The relationship between parent and child, good or bad, has been formed long before, and rules will not change it. What needs to be removed is not the smacking but, as far as possible, the intolerance for the child—the maladjustment in the relationship between parent and child. No rule about smacking will correct this. Smacking of children is practised by apes and is an evolved and established way of guiding children towards the right behaviour patterns.

Emotions, not facts, are basic to our dealings with people

The fact that truth is not absolute matters to people, in that we depend for co-operation on natural affection bonds. Life is based on sympathy and antipathy; these are not logically motivated but come from the nature of each individual, living in her/his own universe with its special set of truths. For instance, small-scale trade is based very much on attitudes between people; you will do business with a person if you trust him or her, and you will have that trust if he/she strikes a chord of sympathy with your own feelings and attitudes. Parents' treatment of children is not logically calculated (Victorian efforts to make it so resulted in stilted, contradictory and unnatural relationships between parents and children) but based on their feelings for that child, like or dislike, acceptance or resentment. The child's whole emotional makeup will be determined by this treatment and will in turn determine its behaviour towards others as an adolescent and adult, which therefore will not be logical either. When marriages break down, it is usually not because one party is feckless, but because one party cannot accept the way the other is, and probably also complains about it. The breakdown is thus on account of attitudes, an emotional and not a rational thing. The good arguer in any domestic disagreement does not dispute along logical lines, but works out in her/his own mind the points that will convince the other of her goodwill. When people who do not

GOODNESS VERSUS TRUTH

know each other very well talk socially, their interest generally is, rather than in the rational content of the other's remarks, in the evidence shown by the other of an attitude favouring the listener, showing liking of her/him and her kind, and agreeing with things that she has said. Charity, or tolerance, is an attitude that stems from a willingness to ignore truth, to be ignorant about people and yet accept them. Henryk Skolimowski writes that "Human history is full of examples of one people not comprehending the views of other people. Instead of condemning those whom we do not understand 'for not knowing any better', we can now say—from the position of the new epistemology—that true understanding means compassion, means understanding that there are different roads leading to reality and to enlightenment... Older spiritual traditions were quite right to insist that compassion is the ability to see reality through the eyes (and hearts) of others... Thus one of the consequences of the new epistemology is tolerance."[8] Charles Darwin, that pioneer of rationalism in biology, wrote to Joseph Hooker: "Talk of fame, honour, pleasure, wealth, are all dirt compared with affection."[9]

The Christian faith, along with other creeds whose ethical teaching is similar, is found by many to be not factually true, and as a result the whole is rejected and its great influence for morality and a charitable attitude to others is lost. If we realized that truth is not absolute and that behaviour towards others is of prime importance, we would find Christianity far more relevant and important and adopt it in our daily lives. By being too logical, we damage our inter-personal relationships. People see that other people are wrong about

EVOLUTION AND THE NATURE OF GOOD

something, and say so, to them or to someone else. This excess of logic militates against the good relations within species which are inherent in nature. Christ's approach was non-logical: Love thy neighbour; love thine enemies; in general, be nice to people whether you think them good or bad. Our failure is in not realizing that the physical world is different to each of us, as I have argued in the previous book; and also, that in Nature, attitudes are not based on defined truth but on feelings that people—and animals—have towards each other. If you do a favour for someone, it is logical to think that next time he/she should do one for you; however by doing it again, willingly and sincerely, you will generate a greater degree of goodwill in that person.

Christianity in fact recognizes the essential non-logic of human thought and relationships: its three cardinal virtues are faith, hope and charity, all of which in their different ways are illogical and do not use scientific-style reasoning.

It is important to understand the difference between the real world and the physical world. The former includes emotions and objectives (that is why it will never be possible to create a human-like robot). For instance, to the physicist the crunching of a rod made of calcium produces a reaction similar to that caused by the crunching of a rod made of carbon. But the effect on you or me of seeing a car run over a person's leg is quite different from seeing it run over the branch of a tree.

The essence to me of the human world around me is my relationship to others—the attitudes that prevail between us. It is a two-sided scenario. Attitudes are unknown to objective physics.

GOODNESS VERSUS TRUTH

Truth is not absolute

In my previous book the conclusion was reached that there is no absolute general truth, but that absolute truth pertains to each individual and is different for each. This realization severely downgrades the value of "truth" as a yardstick for the desirability of any action or attitude, such as asserting the superiority of a particular religion or discriminating against people because of that superiority. Oliver Wendell Holmes Jr., the jurist and legal reformer, who suffered severely in the American Civil War both physically and mentally, had a profound lifelong distrust of absolutes and certainty, and a conviction that "certitude leads to violence".[10] I now find myself loving the things that I no longer believe to be true, because they are associated in some way with goodness. I revel in the beauty of hymns that I sang as a child, their parts and their descants. They were associated with my parents, with good times, good attitudes and good aspirations. It is those associations that make them fine and proper objects to celebrate and enjoy and sing with gusto.

The need for a concept of truth in human society

For any sort of complex interaction between people, the efficient way is to use truth, as an intermediate stage between, first, making observations and collecting data (the input side) and second, making decisions for action. Primitive animals react immediately to stimuli, but those that have developed a cerebral cortex subject the observation to some processing, and as humans have increased the processing, we have come to divide the reaction into two parts, the receiving of information, from which we get what we call truth, and the response, which is our action as a result of that truth.

George Steiner traces the origin of the concept of abstract truth to the ancient Greeks. It "springs up in one place and one place only, and at one specific and singular time in our history. The hunters of abstract truth are, to the best of our knowledge, men of Ionia and of the Greek colonies in southern Italy. Their wondrous infatuation arises at some point between the 7th and 5th centuries BC. It does not arise in any other civilisation or place or time." Those who today pursue abstract truths in the sciences, in mathematics, in philosophy, are "heirs to their hunger."[11]

Although humans defined "truth" with the Greeks less than 3,000 years ago, it has come to be an essential concept in the working of our modern life. Because of the complexity of our lives, truth has come to be seen by developed peoples as a clear entity, and is regarded as a necessary preliminary to taking any sort of action.

The limitations of truth

Science does not meet human needs. François Jacob writes that "The 17th century had the wisdom to introduce reason as a useful and even necessary tool for handling human affairs. The Enlightenment and the 19th century had the folly to consider it not merely necessary but even sufficient for the solution of all problems."[12] In the pursuit of their subject, modern physicists—

with the exception of those few, such as Werner Heisenberg, Erwin Schrödinger, and Arthur Eddington, who have given thought to the philosophical implications of quantum theory— are out-and-out materialists. In other words, they accept as real and absolute the objects in the physical world, and recognize no differences in the universes of individuals. To them there is one all-pervading universe and they set themselves to explore it to its utmost reaches, from the vast to the miniscule, with the object of spreading more widely the frontiers of science and extending our knowledge of what they consider to be ultimate immutable truth. They are trained to handle this absolute universe at all times rationally in accordance with logic and mathematical deduction.

Science does not find absolute truths

The real problems, however, are experienced in the subjective; the real world, as has been discussed above, is that of personal experience, emotions and needs. Our proper objective is to address these original biological essentials; they are not handled by reductionist science, which deals only with relations between things in both physical and biological worlds. Even though it may find a "Band-Aid" type of solution for medical, psychological and social problems, the result is not to restore stability but to make society more complicated and produce daughter problems, examples being antibiotic resistance, depression and heart disease.

E.O. Wilson, the founder of the objective life-science of sociobiology, does not believe that pure knowledge can change the ground rules of human behaviour or alter the

EVOLUTION AND THE NATURE OF GOOD

main course of history's predictable trajectory.[13] According to Michael Polanyi, "Objectivism has totally falsified our conception of truth, by exalting what we can know and prove, while covering up with ambiguous utterances all that we know and cannot prove, even though the latter knowledge underlies, and must ultimately set its seal to, all that we can prove. In trying to restrict our minds to the few things that are demonstrable, and therefore explicitly dubitable, it has overlooked the a-critical choices which determine the whole being of our minds, and has rendered us incapable of acknowledging these vital choices."[14] François Jacob finds value in myths. A myth, he says, has moral content. In a myth, human beings find their law. Science does not find this law; indeed science is an attempt to free investigation and knowledge from human emotional attitudes. "The scientist", writes Jacob, "seeks to remove himself from the world he is endeavouring to understand. He tries to step back, so to speak, to the position of a spectator who is not part of the world under study. By this trick, the scientist hopes to investigate what he considers to be 'the real world around him'. This so-called 'objective world' thus becomes devoid of mind and soul, of joy and sadness, of desire and hope. In brief, this scientific, or 'objective' world is completely dissociated from our familiar world of everyday experience. This attitude underlies the whole network of knowledge developed by Western societies since the Renaissance."[15]

Melvyn Konner points out how poets and classical playwrights see life as it really is but do not try to reason about

GOODNESS VERSUS TRUTH

it, while scientists study it but do not come to grips with its real problems. The literary writings are "totally inconsistent with the fundamental faith of all the tinkerers." Leo Tolstoy wrote in his private notebook: "As soon as a man applies his intelligence and only his intelligence to any object at all, he unfailingly destroys the object."[16] Derek Gjertsen recalls that Epicurus, St. Augustine and Matthew Arnold all found that science did not meet human needs. Keats, William Blake, Kierkegaard and Theodore Roszak found it positively harmful.[17] Furthermore, "Many, today, in the West, find it hard to accept that knowledge about the fundamental nature of reality can easily be obtained by consulting any one of a large number of physics text-books. Such knowledge, they feel, can only be found in distant lands, in Nepal perhaps, from a learned and holy teacher, and can only be acquired when a state of spiritual purity has been achieved."[18] The pioneers of quantum theory saw that classical physics does not solve human problems. To Schrödinger, "Most painful is the absolute silence of all our scientific investigations towards our questions concerning the meaning and scope of the whole display", as seen by "the consciously contemplating, perceiving and feeling subject."[19] Heisenberg sees danger in the spread of the materialist attitude to the developing world. Its rapid extension into countries outside the European tradition, he says, must make itself felt even more strongly than in Europe. "... in many places this new activity must appear as a decline of the older culture, as a ruthless and barbarian attitude, that upsets the sensitive balance on which all human happiness rests."[20]

EVOLUTION AND THE NATURE OF GOOD

Good came first, and was evolved

If man does evil, it is not the fault of his natural endowment.
             Mencius[21]

Ethical behaviour is built into living things. It relates to the interactions between individuals. To achieve optimal survival, members of species have to behave in the way calculated to assist and preserve their fellows, and as a result of natural selection this is what they do. Humans have evolved to an even greater extent to depend completely for survival on co-operation with other people. As a result, Good is the absolute to each one of us; it is the subjective aspect of the objective fact of human relationships. Good embraces all those things that enhanced our ancestors' prospects of survival, most importantly our co-operative, kind and generous behaviour towards other people.

Mary Midgley recognizes the importance of our evolution in shaping our ethical code. "Human morality", she writes, "is not a brute anomaly in the world. Our moral freedom is not something biologically bizarre. No denial of the reality of ethics, nothing offensive to its dignity, follows from accepting our evolutionary origin. To the contrary, human moral capacities are just what could be expected to evolve when a highly social creature becomes intelligent enough to become aware of profound conflicts among its motives."[22]

Iris Murdoch's book *The Sovereignty of Good* consists of three papers published by her in the 1960's. She sees good as the ultimate reality, the important thing rather than truth and science, and presents good as the fundamental, important reality to humans.[23]

Free-will exists, and is subjective

If we did not have free-will there would be little point in writing about ethics, nor of discussing how goodness, or the exercising of ethical behaviour, is the prior concern of living animals including ourselves. The case for free-will was discussed in my previous book;[24] essentially, it exists because our view of the world is subjective, and from that primary vantage-point we are free to choose, as we would not be if we had to view ourselves as part of the physical world, automatons driven by the laws of Nature—which is indeed what we are when seen objectively. Sartre combined the materialism and mechanistic nature of Marxist theory with an "existentialist view of each individual, looking out from behind his own eyes and seeing the world as a field for his own choices, for shaping his own life."[25] Mary Warnock discusses non-predictability and the sense it gives us of a choice of action. From there, she develops the subjective viewpoint: "If we start from where we are, we can see that science is only one among human activities, and the supposed causal, law-like explanations which science seeks ... are not the only kind of explanations. Equally important ... are ... subjective phenomena, the events of people's inner life." The necessary condition of sympathy is central to the very existence of ethics. However, we "can forget the question whether we are free or determined. In real life ... what we do know is that our

EVOLUTION AND THE NATURE OF GOOD

immediate and more generalised reactions to people commit us
to a belief in personal responsibility and thus to ethics."[26]

The question that now arises is: how should we use this free
will?

Chapter 2
Religion and ethics

The need for ethical behaviour has given rise to religious belief among humans, including the three great religions of the Old World, Judaism, Christianity and Islam. In general the message of these religions is: behave well to please God, and earn a heavenly or earthly reward.

The relationship between God and good

At a secular level, fellow-humans and other living things are the foundation of ethics; there is no other potential recipient that could benefit from our good behaviour. If God is introduced into the equation, moral behaviour is extended to serving him as well, in as far as he has an interest in matters other than living things. If God is seen as a force immanent in people or other forms of life, and does not have human characteristics, he (it) still remains a mystery as we do not know its origins, but it becomes identical with good, since the benefit to which it gives rise can only be to living things.

Polytheism and pragmatic religion

As Karen Armstrong points out, the early deities, including the God of the Jewish patriarchs, were conceived largely in the context of: which God should one follow, which will be the most helpful to us? "Israeli belief in God was deeply pragmatic. Abraham and Jacob both put their faith in El because he worked for them: they did not sit down and prove that he existed; El was not a philosophical abstraction. In the ancient world, *mana* [the sense of the 'spiritual' or the 'holy' which pervades the lives of people in more traditional societies at every level and which was once an essential component of our human experience of the world[1]] was a self-evident fact of life and a god proved his worth if he could transmit this effectively. This pragmatism would always be a factor in the history of God. People would continue to adopt a particular conception of the divine because it worked for them, not because it was scientifically or philosophically sound."[2]

Abraham, Isaac and Jacob were probably not monotheists. "Indeed," Armstrong writes, "it is probably more accurate to call these early Hebrews pagans who shared many of their religious beliefs with their neighbours in Canaan. They would certainly have believed in the existence of such deities as Morduk, Baal and Anat. They may not all have worshipped the same deity: it is possible that the God of Abraham, the 'Fear' or 'Kinsman' of Isaac and the 'Mighty One' of Jacob were three separate gods."[3]

RELIGION AND ETHICS

The activities of the gods, like their existence, took the form of myths, and might be changed from time to time.

To the ancients, therefore, effectiveness was the important thing and their God was adapted to this purpose. Truth was not the directing force in life. It is hard for us moderns to imagine that absolute truth was not an important concept for those people, who were not, like us, the intellectual descendants of Aristotle. The falsity of the concept of absolute truth is discussed in my book *Evolution and the Nature of Reality*.[4]

Because *Homo* is a reasoning animal, people have always asked *why* we should behave in the benign way dictated by our community. Various myths, including deities, have been invoked to provide an explanation; but at first they were exchangeable and dispensable and did not suffer from the tyranny of absolute truth which was introduced later.

Karen Armstrong was a nun in a Roman Catholic order and left it. Her book *A History of God* is a study of religions through the ages which is profoundly objective and shows great insight. She highlights the value of myths to ancient people and to those who have not come under the influence of the three great monotheistic religions; she sees truth as secondary to the quest for good. She also shows a deep understanding of human nature, and of the dangers of advancing technology and the acceleration of modern life. Progress, she writes, has become the myth of the western world—its god—and will prove to be at least as fragile as the myths of other ages and places.[5]

It was the acceptance of myths and of gods whose being and behaviour did not have to follow rational rules that enabled

EVOLUTION AND THE NATURE OF GOOD

societies to create and enforce the ethical codes that are so important for their integration and survival. It was in fact not possible until recently to use a rational method to work out a code of behaviour, because not enough was known about the biology or origin of humans. Only since the work of Darwin in the mid-nineteenth century has it been possible to see how this can be done, and the purpose of this book is to link evolution and morality in this way.

Fortunately, we can behave well without esoteric theories. The urge to good behaviour towards one's fellows is inborn and instinctive, and neither in humans nor in other animals is it necessary or even desirable to have a *reason* why we should behave well. We do not therefore have to contend with the unsatisfactory position, adopted by the Greeks and other philosophers over the years, where only the intellectual élite can decide what is best to do. Rational thought, though, has long been part of the human armamentarium, and it is natural that our forebears should have asked questions about how we should behave. The gods and myths of old served them well in providing answers.

Monotheism and the impact of "truth"

When the monotheistic religions were founded they advocated charity, tolerance and compassion. The law of Moses and the teachings of both Jesus and Mohammed were like that; the three religions are very similar in that respect. As church establishments grow and become entrenched there is a

RELIGION AND ETHICS

movement towards dogmatism and liturgy, confrontation with other religions and hostility towards their practitioners.

The concept of truth, invented by the ancient Greeks as a necessary tool for handling complex ideas and situations that could not be resolved without thought, came to be adopted by the three monotheistic religions. The idea of truth, which had previously been applied in a scientific context, establishing absolute mathematical and physical relationships ($2 + 2 = 4$, or ice is less dense than water) was applied by the religious establishments to their myths. They became doctrinal and dogmatic and insisted that their teachings should be accepted literally. This enthronement of truth has been the cause of much intolerance and persecution.

In the seventh century BC King Josiah of Israel, concluding that the threat posed by the empire-building King of Babylon had been brought upon his people by their widespread worship of several pagan gods, ordered the destruction of all their altars. From now on the God of Israel, Yaweh, was to be the only God who might be worshipped. The historical books of Joshua, Judges, Samuel and Kings were revised according to the new ideology, making Yaweh the author of a holy war of extermination in Canaan, and Joshua his bloodthirsty agent. "The dangers of such theologies of election, which are not qualified by the transcendent perspective of an Isiah, are clearly shown in the holy wars that have scarred the history of monotheism. Instead of making God a symbol to challenge our prejudice and force us to contemplate our own shortcomings, it can be used to endorse our egotistic hatred and make it absolute.

It makes God behave exactly like us, as though he were simply another human being."[6]

The Christian insistence on dogma was renewed in earnest in the 11th century. The appalling cruelties of the Crusades and the successive Inquisitions were the direct result of it, and triumphed over the natural human instinct for compassion. The same attitude survives to the present day: orthodox (fundamentalist) Christians blame us for what we believe as well as for what we do, and we are told by many of the Christian churches that unless we are converted we will suffer the tortures of Hell. As a footnote, the logic of this Christian militarism is flawed. It is impossible to control what one believes; faith is entirely a gift to the individual subject, experienced from within, and those who do not have it do not merit punishment or correction.

Buddhism

Buddhism comes closer than Judaism, Christianity or Islam in reconciling the rational nature of events observed in the world with a religion which dictates moral behaviour appropriate to humans. The moral code it derives, in turn, is appropriate to the nature of human needs as found from a study of our evolutionary and social history.

Buddhism had its origins in Brahmanism, which was the complex sacrificial religion that arose in post-Vedic India about 900 BC. During the eighth to fifth centuries BC, sages issued treatises called the Upanishads, which evolved a distinctive

RELIGION AND ETHICS

conception of the godhood Brahman that transcends the gods but is found to be intimately present in all things. Brahman was the inner meaning of all existence. Brahman cannot be addressed as "thou". It does not speak to mankind. "It does not respond to us in a personal way: sin does not 'offend' it and it cannot be said to 'love' us or be 'angry'. Thanking or praising it for creating the world would be entirely inappropriate." [7] In this way belief in Brahman removes the great stumbling-block inherent in Judaism, Christianity and Islam, all of which worship a God endowed with human characteristics who loves, approves and disapproves, and judges, and so cannot be reconciled with a world dominated by rationality.

The ascetic Siddhartha Gautama, usually referred to as "The Buddha", founded Buddhism in the 6th century BC as a reaction against the sacrificial religion of the current orthodox Brahmanism. He preached Dharma, the truth about right living, which alone could free us from pain. He "taught that it was possible to gain release from *dhukka* [painful living] by living a life of compassion for all living beings, speaking and behaving gently, kindly and accurately and refraining from anything like drugs or intoxicants that cloud the mind." This lifestyle will lead to *nirvana*, a state of lasting, secure bliss and happiness.

"Effectiveness rather than philosophical or historical demonstration has always been the hallmark of a successful religion," says Armstrong. "... for centuries Buddhists in many parts of the world have found that this lifestyle does yield a sense of transcendent meaning... Experience was the only reliable proof.

EVOLUTION AND THE NATURE OF GOOD

"The Buddha held that the theology or beliefs that a person held, like the ritual he took part in, were unimportant... The only thing that counted was the good life; if it were attempted, Buddhists would find that the Dharma was true, even if they could not express this truth in logical terms."[8] The Buddha's approach is similar to that of the Greek and Roman writers who found living virtuously to be its own reward in this life. It is in sharp contrast to that of Jesus, who in the Sermon on the Mount (Matthew chapter 4) emphasized the reward of entering the Kingdom of Heaven as the prize for virtuous behaviour. Peter Singer remarks that "The dominance of Christian teaching in Western ethics may well have been responsible for the decline of the assumption that living well brings its own reward in this life."[9]

Buddhism is therefore a non-aggressive, tolerant and charitable religion, not personalizing God, placing responsibility on the individual, and creating an ethical system consistent with the findings of Darwin and more recent work on human evolution.

Ethics without dogmatic religion

Attempts to separate ethics from religious faith date back to ancient times. During the Han dynasty in China, Confucianism was recognized as the state philosophy, and it was the Confucian understanding of "right conduct" that governed everything. The Chinese imagined the universe as an ordered whole, and they had no creation myth and no creator-lawgiver who was

RELIGION AND ETHICS

supernatural. The elaborate college of Confucian experts ensured that the emperor always behaved in the "right" way.[10] Neo-Confucianism was assembled as a philosophy in the 12th century AD by Zhu Xhi from the writings of several 11th-century thinkers. It recognized a central rational principle in the universe, *li*, which explains both moral behaviour and matter.[11] The Hinayana Buddhists of the second century AD, splitting from the Mahayana school which had come to regard the Buddha and other "enlightened ones" as deities, took a broad philosophical view and held that their beliefs were essentially an ethical system.[12]

Richard Holloway, a bishop in the Church of England, has explored the possibility of deriving a universal moral code that does not depend on the wishes of a particular God.[13] He disappoints however in not recognizing the evolutionary origin of morality and the direction in which it should point us. He does not see an innate drive in humans to behave co-operatively and unselfishly. He shows no concern about the rapidly increasing pace of life—in fact he seems quite to favour technological advance and the acceleration that it produces.

Yet there *are* many parallels between Christian morality, as well as that of other major religions, and ethical views based on our biological history. The most important is, perhaps, that the moral code dictated by biological reasoning, as outlined in Chapter 3, is very close to that taught by Judaism, by Christ, and by Islam. The gospel of Jesus was a gospel of love, in the sense of charity or tolerance. It takes humility, a Christian virtue, to appreciate that the evolution of species, including *Homo*, is cyclical, each rising to prosperity and falling to extinction over a long period. The spread of tolerance and humility will enable this process in humans to last as long as possible, and more important, to occur gracefully and naturally without intolerable stresses on individuals. As a final point of similarity, in essence prayer and personal moral wrangling are the same thing.

We cannot really do away with religion in framing an ethical code. This chapter began with a claim that God can be defined as the essence of good, and that the motive force for good comes from within us. It is not thought out and is not rational, and in that sense it is a form of religion or faith.

The impact of rationalism

All the three major monotheistic religions have encountered and had to deal with the advent of rationalism, which stemmed from Aristotle and the other Greek thinkers. In the fourth century BC the Jews came under its influence when the Greeks began to colonise Asia and Africa and founded city-states in Tyre, Sidon, Gaza and elsewhere. The author of the book of Proverbs, writing in the third century BC, suggested that wisdom was the masterplan that God had devised when he created the world. In the first century BC, in *The Wisdom of Solomon*, a Jew of Alexandria warned Jews to resist the seductive Hellenic culture. Soon afterwards the Jewish philosopher Philo, who was strongly influenced by Plato, tried to turn the historical books of the Bible into elaborate allegories, since if taken literally they would be irrational.[14]

RELIGION AND ETHICS

During the ninth century AD the Arabs came into contact with Greek science and philosophy and studied astronomy, alchemy, medicine and mathematics with such success that they became world leaders in science. A rational philosophy emerged, called *falsafah*, whose practitioners— the Faylasufs—aimed to live rationally in accordance with the laws that they believed governed the cosmos; rationalism, they claimed, had evolved a higher notion of God than the revealed God of scripture. In the tenth century two sects which arose from these *falasa* origins, the Mutazilis and the Asharites, to quote Armstrong, "attempted, in different ways, to connect the religious experience of God with ordinary rational thought. .. Muslims were trying to find out whether it was possible to talk about God as about other matters... the Greeks had decided on balance that it was not and that silence was the only appropriate form of theology. Ultimately most Muslims would come to the same conclusion... Like Christianity and Judaism, Islam ... had collided with the Greek rationalism in the Hellenic centres of the Middle East."[15]

It is the Christian faith, most of all, that has tried to reconcile religion with the rationality of the Greeks and has insisted on a catalogue of facts and a creed that must be accepted as the first condition of fellowship with God, and hence with good. Armstrong writes that in the fourth century AD, "a dogmatic intolerance was creeping into Christianity, which would ultimately make the adoption of the 'correct' or orthodox symbols crucial and obligatory. This doctrinal obsession [is] unique to Christianity ..."[16] With the rapid advance of science in the seventeenth century the great thinkers of western Europe, including Descartes, Newton, Voltaire and Spinoza, were forced to accept a rational philosophy. All of these men believed in God; none were what today we would call an atheist. Much effort was put into fitting God into a rational view of the world. However, as long as God was seen to have human characteristics that was to prove impossible.

The result of this insistence on dogma is that Christians today find themselves in a catch-22 situation; they have to choose between fundamentalism and hypocrisy. The first is an honest position: fundamentalists accept the facts laid down by the Church and give them priority over all conclusions reached by scientific or other rational means. The great majority of Christians, however, profess their belief in a man-like God, the divinity of Christ, the Trinity and the miracles related in the New Testament; but at the same time they believe in science and use rational thought, even though it has become clear that the two approaches are irreconcilable.

The transition from a man-like God to God as the essence of goodness

Some seventeenth century philosophers, notably Voltaire, saw God as having created the whole cause-and-effect system by which the world was now perceived to work, in which, once started, he does not interfere nor disrupt its running. He is not external but immanent. To Voltaire morality and not dogma was the essence of God, and a religion that was cruel was absurd.[17] Spinoza went further: not only is God immanent, but Spinoza was close to the idea that God is anything that does the job of leading to good, and does not have to have human-like behaviour.[18]

It is only a short step from the standpoint of Voltaire and Spinoza to see God as synonymous with good. The difficulty with this idea arises because Christians and other monotheists insist that God has human characteristics: he observes, thinks, loves, grieves and judges. It is irrational to think that God should have the characteristics of humans, one only of the millions of species that he has put in the world.

It is by shaking off the deeply ingrained belief that any God must think like a man or woman that the true nature of God can be discerned. What is left then is the essence of good, the spirit that inspires people to behave well. That spirit, the urge to co-operation and mutual help, is inborn in all of us. The various myths of the past have helped people, as they have come to seek reasons for everything, to fulfil this obligation to others. The new myth of human evolution, which requires people to help each other—or in other words, to be good—should serve us well at the present time.

The soul

Peter Watson concludes his massive book *Ideas*, which comprehensively and with skilful analysis traces the history of

EVOLUTION AND THE NATURE OF GOOD

thought from prehistoric times to the beginning of the twentieth century, with a consideration of consciousness and of our failure to reach an understanding of it. The romantics of the nineteenth century, including painters, poets and musicians, were dissatisfied with the materialistic mode of thought that had grown up with the advance of science and industry. They felt the need for some more worth-while way of living, and sought it within themselves, claiming that "… everything we value in life, morality above all, comes from within… The romantics in particular show very clearly the idea of the evolution of the soul."[19]   The idea of the soul is in fact the recognition of our inner urges to co-operation and moral behaviour, which cannot be embraced in the materialistic philosophy of the scientists and industrialists. This soul has been bequeathed to us by ancestors who could not have survived without it.   But it is strictly subjective and gives rise to instinctive behaviour. While science has been enormously successful in explaining the world outside ourselves, "man's study of himself is his biggest intellectual failure in history, his least successful area of enquiry."[20]   Watson is referring here not to objective studies such as psychology and sociology, but to consciousness and the moral sense. Our failure in that respect is not surprising.   As I have discussed previously,[21] we start life subjectively, with no idea of the causal way in which events unfold, and only by degrees build up a picture of the physical world; but the ingredients of our consciousness and moral sense are born with us and do not depend on the outside world. That is the nature of our soul. We can never find a rational explanation for consciousness because it is a given; as Gödel's theorem asserts, no system can explain itself. In the case of the moral sense, however, although it impels us through its subjective and instinctive nature, we have found an explanation for it by scientific means, through the observations of Darwin; people have survived because they helped each other.

Conclusion

The essence of goodness is charity, kindness and co-operation, and it is extended to a lesser extent to other animals and even to plants—we live in an ecosphere in which living things all support each other.

The spur to goodness, thus defined, in each human, comes from within ourselves: we are evolved to co-operate, in the interest of species survival. It does not require rational thought to produce good behaviour.

However, as our species has learned to reason—in order to improve its position in the world vis-à-vis other species—it has come to ask what is the rational basis for deciding what good behaviour is. As the impetus is inside us and instinctive, we cannot give an explanation; hence myths arise, and these myths have been necessary to satisfy the inquirers and ensure moral behaviour.

In this book I offer yet another myth, that the urge to goodness is explained by our evolutionary history. Whether this myth is accepted or not, it is no more essential to ethical conduct than the other myths, because good behaviour, co-operation,

EVOLUTION AND THE NATURE OF GOOD

charity and kindness are within us and instinctive, and we need only follow our natural inclinations (sometimes after discarding culturally-acquired hostility and hatred) to do what is right.

Chapter 3
Finding a basis for ethics

The purpose of the discipline of Ethics is to decide what we ought to do. It differs from other forms of the pursuit of knowledge—the sciences and philosophy—in that many of its devotees believe that there is no rational basis for it, that one cannot use known facts to derive proper behaviour; in eight words, following Hume, you cannot get an "ought" from an "is". The object of this chapter is to show that there *is* a rational basis for choosing a moral code, and that it lies in the ancestry of mankind.

The search for personal fulfilment

For Epicurus, pleasure was the ultimate end, but he advocated a simple life to achieve this. Aristotle's aim was happiness, which he saw not simply as pleasure, but as an active life that involves the pursuit of philosophical wisdom. The Buddha described the purpose of the good life as "the ceasing of woe".[1]

Jeremy Bentham, the founding father of utilitarianism, was in no doubt that happiness is what we should aim for. John Stuart Mill was his godson, as well as a supporter of his utilitarian philosophy, but held an opposing view: "It is better to be a human being dissatisfied than a pig satisfied; better to be Socrates dissatisfied than a fool satisfied."[2]

The loss of satisfaction and challenge resulting from hedonistic objectives

As long ago as the third century BC, Epicurus appreciated the need for variation in the level of happiness that one enjoys: "And since pleasure is the first good and natural to us, for this very reason we do not choose every pleasure, but sometimes we pass over many pleasures, when greater discomfort accrues to us as a result of them: and similarly we think many pains better than pleasures, since a greater pleasure comes to us when we have endured pains for a long time… we must form our judgement on all these matters." The poorest have the sweetest pleasure in luxury, and to them "plain savours bring a pleasure equal to a luxurious diet … To grow accustomed therefore to simple and not luxurious diet gives us health to the full …" Simple sensuality, to Epicurus, is not pleasure.[3] The significance of this "paradox of hedonism" for socialization is referred to on page 82.

In present-day terms, you could say that it is better to sleep on a hard, kapok-filled mattress than on an inner-sprung mattress. You sleep just as well on the former, it is your norm; you are no less happy. But to visit a friend and have a night on a sprung mattress is a special treat. Likewise it is better to own a black-and-white television set than a coloured one, or a standard car rather than a luxury model. The background level of happiness in one's life is not affected by the texture of the mattress, the colour of the TV, or the silent comfortable acceleration of the car.

This is an important principle to consider in relation to the nature of happiness. It does not result from the accrual of more and more possessions or wealth; any permanent addition to these soon becomes one's norm. This fact has a direct bearing on the acceleration of modern human life, and on the increasing, environmentally destructive use and wastage of resources in the belief that accumulating them will bring greater happiness. The economist Henry Clay wrote: "The rich *as a class* are no happier and no better than the poor *as a class*."[4]

Aldous Huxley presents us with the Brave New World of perfect contentment without fluctuations; he exposes the total abolition of challenge as a mis-representation of happiness. The story is also a protest against the softening-up of our lives, making us less fit for a natural environment.[5]

Aesthetic appreciation

In opposition to the idea that a hedonistic way of life gives the greatest satisfaction, G E Moore emphasizes beauty, which he regards as providing fulfilment to people, and indeed as an absolute good in itself—even when there is no possibility of anyone ever experiencing it.[6] The amount of time, effort and money expended on cultural pursuits such as art and music is witness to the importance that modern humans attach to beautiful things.

EVOLUTION AND THE NATURE OF GOOD

Human relationships

Moore also values friendship—a recognition of the role of interaction between people in producing happiness.[6] Every family member, every lover and every friend knows that much of what we want from life, and of the source of our happiness, has nothing to do with material possessions or pleasant personal sensations, but depends on our relationships with other people. Indeed we are utterly dependent on others; as John Donne wrote, no man is an island.

The role of reason in ethics

Kant believed that morality comes from reason itself. It is true that if ethics is derived through rationality, there must be some *reason* for good behaviour, some definable good that will be identified by a process of reasoning. Kant recognized an innate urge in people to behave well towards one another, and he wanted to show that it is profoundly irrational to act in a manner that is contrary to what you know is right. The obligation to be rational, and to do what one knows to be right, was his "categorical imperative". He wrote: "Act so that you treat humanity, whether in your own person or that of another, always as an end and never as a means only."[7] He was, however, unable to set out the deductive process required to determine what that right behaviour is. As Mary Warnock says, "... the doctrine of the categorical imperative will not really do, as an explanation of where ethics comes from. Its weakness lies in its separation of reason from all other human faculties and propensities."[8] Kant was working from a "given" that he could not explain; the innate urge to co-operate and help. Once that "given" is accepted, his approach was strictly rational. His failure to find a rationale for moral behaviour is not surprising since he lived before the time of Darwin and the other nineteenth-century pioneers of evolutionary theory; he did not have access to the biological basis needed for finding one. Recognition of the role of human evolution in determining our behaviour and our need for co-operation supplies the reason that Kant was missing.

Kant's concept of duty for duty's sake highlights the importance of obligations between people, and provides a link with the later biological ideas of kin selection, group cooperation, and the need of humans for each others' help.

The spontaneous human urge to behave cooperatively

We have necessarily acquired a deep instinct to help each other. There is a long line of thought that finds the source of ethics in the attitudes of benevolence and sympathy for others that most people have.[9]

There appear to be some very general basic principles which are recognized at least implicitly to some extent in all societies. J.L.Mackie believes that people judge things to be right or wrong "because something about those things arouses certain responses immediately in them ... 'Moral sense' or 'intuition' is

EVOLUTION AND THE NATURE OF GOOD

an initially more plausible description of what supplies many of our basic moral judgments than 'reason'."[10]

Several other authors hold that moral values come from within the individual, including David Hume, Edward Westermarck, A.J Ayer, and Jean-Paul Sartre.[11] None of these, however, believe that these values can be derived by reasoning; they do not recognize a biological origin for them.

Service to others

Whether "good" consists of happiness, variety, physical or mental activity, aesthetic appreciation, happy relations with other people, or something else, it is clearly something that affects *people*. It would be impossible to think of a good that exists in the absence of living things. Ethics is the discipline that tries to define how a person should behave so as to help—maximise the "good" enjoyed by—other people and animals, and it is therefore concerned with relationships, especially human relationships.

Gandhi supports *ahisma*, the Hindu principle of harmlessness, as the goal. To achieve self-purification one has to become absolutely passion-free in thought, speech and action. Ahisma is the furthest limit of humility.[12]

Jesus advocated total and unreserved altruism, in return for a heavenly reward. His teaching goes beyond "tit-for-tat", referred to in Chapter 1, which modern computer experiments have shown to be the most effective system for co-operation; that is, start by being helpful, and thereafter respond in kind

FINDING A BASIS FOR ETHICS

to the helpful or antagonistic attitude of the other party. In Jesus' time (as now) it was the value of altruism that needed emphasizing. His doctrine included: turn the other cheek if a man hits you on one; if he forces you to walk a mile with him, go with him another mile.

Willing service to others results from satisfactory *attitudes* between people—it is not simply a measure of how much pleasure *in toto* is achieved, or how much one person owes to another, nor yet is it the result of an unemotional, diffuse benevolence to the whole of mankind.

Utilitarianism

The aim of utilitarianism, founded in the latter part of the eighteenth century by Jeremy Bentham, is to achieve the greatest good for the greatest number of people. Its benevolence is directed at the whole of humanity, without recognizing a variation in obligation dependent on the closeness of the kinship or social relationship between the people concerned.

The obvious weakness of the utilitarian approach is that it is impossible for an individual to measure the amount of pleasure that her/his actions will produce in other people at varying degrees of remoteness from herself. "If we are not able to compare experiences in respect of pleasure," writes Ewing, "utilitarianism cannot be applied at all ...".[13] In spite of his role as a co-founder with Bentham of utilitarianism, J.S.Mill saw one of its shortcomings: "What is there to decide whether a

EVOLUTION AND THE NATURE OF GOOD

particular pleasure is worth purchasing at the cost of a particular pain, except the feelings and judgment of the experienced?"[14]

Henry Sidgwick writes that it is difficult to compare the pleasures and pains of others with our own—and "a comparison of either with the pleasures and pains of brutes is obviously still môre obscure." It is also difficult to consider the interests of posterity. Finally, we cannot calculate what overall result our actions will produce in the way of universal pain or pleasure.[15]

In short, it is hugely difficult to calculate optimal utilitarian behaviour. The problems include estimation of pleasure/pain; what will make for best interests in the future; interests of others further out who are affected; and the great difficulty of knowing what "best interests" means.

The relevance of human evolution to the study of ethics

In mainstream Ethics evolution has had little consideration. The debate has been largely concerned with the conflict between utilitarianism—that is, achieving the greatest happiness for the greatest number—and duty for duty's sake, the "categorical imperative" proposed by Kant.

Voices raised against the significance of evolution to ethics

Among those who believe that evolution has no moral message for us are François Jacob,[16] S.J. Gould,[17] and G.E. Moore, who argued, like Hume, that you could not get an "ought" from an "is"—that you could not derive morality from the facts of human behaviour.[18]   Ewing discusses "naturalistic" views of ethics in general, and dismisses the natural sciences as a source of ethical guidance; he regards psychology as the chief science to be considered. "Another biological definition proffered of good or right", he says, "is 'in conformity with evolutionary development'." But he dismisses this.[19] Mel Thompson rejects the "natural law" theory of ethics.[20] He evidently feels that it commits one to a teleological attitude: "The 'natural law' theory of ethics is based on [Aristotle's] idea of final causes and the corresponding 'good' towards which all things are designed to work."[21] For Robert Winston, "There is no logical reason why there is anything morally worthwhile about the process of natural selection; it is, by its very nature, morally neutral, a biological process based on random mutations."[22]

Misunderstanding of the role of evolution

A number of writers have rejected the idea that our evolutionary history has a role in determining what we should do for the reason that they see it only as "the survival of the fittest", and do not consider the great part that socialization has played in recent human evolution. Some are concerned that the nature which evolution has passed down to us is violently competitive and anti-social, and must be opposed. T.H. Huxley wrote: "The practice of that which is ethically best—what we call goodness or virtue—involves a course of conduct which in all respects is opposed to that which leads to success in the cosmic struggle for existence."[23] Tolstoy complained that Darwinism (Gould's words) "undermines morality by claiming that success in nature can only be measured by victory in bloody battle—the 'struggle for existence' or 'survival of the fittest' to cite Darwin's own choice of mottoes."[24] Erwin Schrödinger believes that "... our conscious life ... is necessarily a continued fight against our primitive ego... consciousness and discord with one's own self are inseparably linked up ...".[25] E.O. Wilson says we have to know about our inherited nature so as to overcome it and make ourselves fit our recently developed culture.[26]

The concept of the survival of the fittest has been misapplied to modern human culture by some people who regard westernization as an ideal to be aimed at, in order to prove their superiority to other peoples and their right to claim privilege over them or otherwise abuse them. Alvin Toffler writes of influential French right-wing groups who "... argue that races are born unequal and should be kept that way by social policy. They lace their arguments with references to E.O. Wilson and Arthur Jensen to lend supposedly scientific colour to their virulently antidemocratic biases."[27] Stephen Boyden draws attention to this error: "There have, of course, been some isolated attempts to look at human society in terms of biological principles. Perhaps the most notorious of these was Social Darwinism—the intellectual movement initiated by Herbert Spencer which assumed that the evolutionary principles annunciated by Charles Darwin applied not only to biological systems but also to human society, and that a societal organization which was based on the principle of the 'survival of the fittest' was therefore 'natural', and consequently desirable... As in the case of other biological or organic analogies, this concept was based on the false premise that principles which apply to one kind of system (e.g. a certain type of biological system) are applicable to a totally different kind of system (e.g. industrial society)."[28]

Gould agrees that the assumption that natural selection can teach ethical theory as applied to modern societies "has abetted a panoply of social evils that ideologues falsely read into nature from their beliefs—eugenics and (misnamed) social Darwinism are among them."[29] But Gould does not see any opposite positive, socializing role for evolution. He says "... nature ... provides no basis for our moral values."[30] He thus denies not only that our inherited nature makes us brutal and selfish, but also that it makes us mutually helpful.

Support for the role of evolution in ethics

Most of those who have thought and written about morals have sought inspiration about proper conduct out of the air, rather than relating it to the context of real life. The belief that an "ought" cannot be derived from an "is" is widespread. Wilson comments that "Philosophers ... examine the precepts of ethical systems with reference to their consequences and not their origins."[31] There is a great reluctance to accept the animal origins of our behaviour; animals are thought of as amoral and predatory. Mary Midgley expresses the essential dilemma of ethics: "On the one side, we must surely reject the crude, mechanistic, reductive accounts of motive which have so often accompanied insistence on our animal origin, and the fatalism that goes with them. But I think that we have to reject, just as strongly, the no less unreal vision of an antiseptically isolated human essence, a purely spiritual or intellectual pilot arbitrarily set in a physical vehicle which plays no part in his or her motivation."[32]

Throughout the ages there have been those who see human origins as a guide to the framing of an ethical code. Although Aristotle saw moral behaviour as *de novo* in people, to Plato it was a basic strategy for survival. "... from Plato onwards", writes Thompson, "we have seen that some philosophers hold that there are certain principles and values which may be derived from the examination of human beings, their society, and their place within the world as a whole..."[33] Henri Bergson (1859-1941) in *Creative Evolution*, felt that you should act in a way that enables you to follow the stream of evolutionary life in the direction of the future—that you should do nothing to impede the progress of evolution.[34] In Chapter 3 of *The Descent of Man*, Darwin makes it clear that he sees the inherited evolution of social responsibility in animals and *Homo* as the source of the moral sense.[35] Midgley, unlike most modern writers on ethics, recognizes the importance of our evolution in shaping our ethical code.[36]

None of the contributors or discussion participants in Leonard Katz' book *Evolutionary Origins of Morality*[37] have any hesitation in relating morality to humans' evolutionary past.

FINDING A BASIS FOR ETHICS

Humans co-operate naturally

The evolution of humans and their immediate ancestors the hominids—before culture became predominant—has, under the great environmental pressures of the last five million years, been towards increasing mutual help and cooperation. Such cooperation is used not only against the physical environment, but also to cope with the biological environment of the species, in the form of both food and predators. It is not hard to believe that ideally our individual aims should be consistent with this trend, that is, towards more and more interaction, and towards the identification and meeting of felt needs in other people. Gould refers to the Russian writer on social philosophy—and revolutionary anarchist—Petr Kropotkin, who promoted a vision of small cooperative communities setting their own standards. "Kropotkin argues, in his cardinal premise, that the struggle for existence usually leads to mutual aid rather than combat as the chief criterion for evolutionary success. Human society must therefore build upon our natural inclinations (not reverse them, as Huxley held) in formulating a moral order that will bring both peace and prosperity to our species." Gould quotes Kropotkin: "Sociability is as much a law of nature as mutual struggle."[38] Although Gould says that this has got Kropotkin generally regarded as "daftly idiosyncratic", his argument is sound. Humans have developed the cooperative side of animal behaviour to a very great extent—none of us could live alone— and this is deeply embedded in our nature and is the way we

EVOLUTION AND THE NATURE OF GOOD

have to behave in order to survive and maintain maximum stability.

The doctrine of the "naturalistic fallacy"

The prevailing attitude of philosophers about ethics is that, as Hume originally claimed, "You cannot derive as 'ought' from an 'is'." According to this view, rational thinking, which is suitable for handling the way things occur in the physical world as we observe it, cannot be applied to the question of how we should behave. That, it is held, is a feeling, something that arises within each of us, and no-one can gainsay another about it. It is referred to as the subjectivist view.

Alexander Rosenberg says that you cannot ground morality on science for this reason. He thinks evolution does not teach us morality because scoundrels do "better than anyone else, both in terms of well-being and in terms of eventual fitness-maximization".[39] (Rosenberg does not appear to be aware of the role socialization plays in the success—in the sense of predominance – of socialized species.)

Matt Ridley uses a "selfish gene" approach to prove that there is really no such thing as altruism, and that all unselfish behaviour is because it is ultimately to the advantage of the doer. Ridley seems to think that other mammals, even the apes, have very little social sense and cooperate very little. He believes that humans are quite different from animals, and unique in our socialization.[40] To him, co-operation is an essential part of human nature, but it has been specially developed by *Homo* and not by the other "higher" mammals. In this, he says, Kropotkin was wrong.[41]

G E Moore (1873-1958) believed that ethical facts could not be natural facts, and that therefore ethical knowledge could not be obtained by reasoning from observed facts, but must rest on intuition. He was the author of the concept of the "naturalistic fallacy", now widely endorsed by philosophers, which holds that any attempt to derive moral direction from known facts of nature is erroneous.

The "naturalistic fallacy" concept is itself a fallacy

If it is accepted that humans are a product of their evolution, and not merely (retrospective) observers of it, the "naturalistic fallacy" idea must be abandoned. Consideration of our evolution provides a way in which what *should be* can be related to what *is*.

As I have discussed in *Evolution and the nature of reality*,[42] we have no knowledge outside our experience, which experience includes not only that encountered during our lifetime, but also the inherited experience of our ancestors which gives rise to our instinctive behaviour. Our inherited instinct is to help and co-operate with our fellow humans. Conversely, there is no basis unrelated to inherited and acquired experience for knowing what we ought to do. Any attempt to seek one is akin to dogmatism—a declaration that we should behave in such-and-such a way because of some assumed reality such as a God or gods. Kant's *duty as an absolute good* is one form of such dogmatism. Mary Warnock comments on the view of G E

Moore that there are no grounds for moral judgments or moral decisions. She writes: "One might be forgiven for thinking that Moore's doctrine would make sense only to those who held that moral qualities were supernatural, emanating from God. Or somehow from beyond or outside the natural world. For unless one held that faith, what other grounds for the moral could there possibly be except the nature of things, and especially the nature of human beings who alone have a use for the concepts of morality?"[43]

In effect, therefore, to hold to the doctrine of the naturalistic fallacy—by denying that our instinct to nurture the interests of others is our only ethical guide—is to support a dogma, a belief outside the scope of rational thought. There is no criterion for what is good except the benefit of humans or other animals and perhaps plants (we eat them); we share our genes with them and so are compelled to co-operate with them.

Morality is the result of our inborn concern for other people and animals. It is based entirely on *feeling*, an inherited characteristic, and, as has been discussed above, deals with our relations with other sentient beings. Its academic study therefore falls entirely within the realm of biology and anthropology. It is only because we are concerned about others that we feel the need to know what we ought to do.

The obligation of humans to people of other races

Although there are minor differences between human races, the application of laws and practices resulting from the development of culture has to be made without discrimination because the whole species is so similar. People may legitimately favour those closer to them genetically, and those with whom they co-operate closely, but the culture, through the law, must ensure that all such groups have an equal opportunity of promoting their interests.

Our obligation to animals

Both Aquinas and Kant held that it is not necessary to be kind to animals, because they are not rational. Descartes was the chief proponent of the view that animals cannot even feel pain. Appalling cruelties, resulting from such attitudes, have been committed against animals over the ages. [44]

But humans do not have a special place among animals or a right to be thought of differently. Darwin's theory undermines the traditional idea that human life has a special, unique worth. [45] Human dignity rests on the claim that humans are special in some way, e.g. they are made in the image of God. If that is not true, the evidence for human dignity falls away. "From a Darwinian perspective," writes James Rachels in *Created from Animals*, "both the image of God thesis and the rationality thesis [claiming that reasoning makes humans a unique species] are suspect ... there are good Darwinian reasons for thinking it unlikely that any other support for human dignity can be found. [46] ... The main thesis of this book is that Darwinism leads inevitably to the abandonment of the idea of human dignity and substitution of a different sort of ethic."[47] There is, he says, no qualitative difference between animals and humans.[48]

An obligation to animals must therefore be embraced in our ethical code. As will be argued in Chapter 6, our obligation to others is not uniform: it is greatest to those closest to us genetically and in terms of co-operation. Animals, especially some such as farm stock and pets, come quite high on the latter scale.

Only one animal needs a discipline called Ethics

Animals are naturally ethical. An essential—perhaps the most fundamental—point about an approach to ethics is the need to reverse the traditional idea that humans, because they are thinking beings, are thereby the only ones capable of developing ethical behaviour.

The truth is that each species has and observes ethics appropriate to itself, and the development of culture distorts this. The problem of weakness of will applies only to rational beings such as humans.[49] Temptation and the resisting of it are the new elements that have arisen in humans, making ethics a recognizable discipline. Singer suggests "that we abandon the assumption that ethics is uniquely human... Philosophical systems of ethics are highly sophisticated elaborations of more widespread concepts which have themselves evolved from prehuman social behaviour."[50]

Humans, the most cultured of animals, have had their ethical system severely perverted, and the main agency of this has been the emergence of competition—business, trade, shares, wealth, the concept of property—as the basis of maintaining our society. This has given us an essentially selfish attitude instead of the naturally co-operative way of relating to each other. One might look at it this way: our naturally sharing ideal has become limited to our immediate families, perhaps through a stage of continued sharing with more extended families when we were more dependent on them. The use of extended families is mentioned in Chapters 4 and 8.

Ethics had to be invented for humans

The development of temptation comes with culture. With temptation comes the need to resist it. i.e. behave decently and appropriately towards other members of the species. Humans, having an advanced culture, have developed an academic discipline of ethics to study this question. Ethical behaviour is not a human innovation, but ethical study has been found necessary because of our deviations from it.

The idea widely promoted by philosophers, that ethical behaviour is a human invention, enabling us to act in a way that will help our peers as well as ourselves, is therefore misguided. Humans have had to formalize morality because of their great culturally-generated capacity for violating normal decent animal relations. The truth is that an appropriate morality exists for each species. We should be considering *deviations* from it, or *immorality*, and how culture has rendered this a particularly acute problem with humans.

PART II
THE INTERDEPENDENCE OF PEOPLE

Chapter 4
The origins of co-operation

Ever since single-celled organisms joined together to form metazoa, co-operation has been the key to the survival of living things, and as organisms have become more complex, so has co-operation become more important. The forms of co-operation that are important to humans today have been inherited from our mammalian ancestors. The earliest and most deeply-entrenched one is the care of mothers for their children; then comes the relationship between sex partners; then other kin; then the whole local community, then the whole species. Humans have carried this further, and recognize their obligation to domestic and farm animals, and more recently the whole range of living things including plants as, with the belated realization that we are destroying our means of survival, we acknowledge our responsibility to the ecosphere.

THE ORIGINS OF CO-OPERATION

While this chapter aims to explain the importance of co-operation as the foundation of ethical behaviour, it also points up the ways in which we can contribute or fail to contribute to such co-operation and which in this way provide a moral yardstick.

The mother-child relationship

The importance of women

The hand that rocks the cradle
Is the hand that rules the world.
    William Ross Wallace, 1865

Women, in their evolved role as mothers, carers, peacemakers and maintainers of stability rather than as competitors, are seriously underrated in the modern world.

In scientific usage, we unconsciously emphasize the central importance of the female in our language, by referring to "daughter bacteria", "daughter cysts" etc. In common language, ships, cars, and other vehicles are called "she", as are countries and other institutions. Natural selection recognizes the pre-eminence of women in the legacies it has left to us. Not only are men more likely than women to be killed in accidents, but they are also more prone to disease, because women have to remain fit and healthy to look after children.[1] In crowded and trying circumstances, Carl Sagan and Ann Druyan write, the female's role in improving relations is crucial. Among apes, "Especially under crowded conditions, females play a central role in encouraging and helping to implement coups d'etat."[2] The authors "can't help wondering

EVOLUTION AND THE NATURE OF GOOD

what would happen if women played a role in world politics proportionate to their numbers."[3] Women, instead of joining the rat-race, could use their energies towards establishing viable alternatives to masculine forms of power. There is no good reason for women to push for equal opportunity to serve in Titan missile silos or as bomber pilots or to build advanced nuclear weapons.[4] If women, especially family women, were represented pro-rata (i.e. equally with men) in assemblies of militant groups such as (to choose examples current at the time of writing) the parties to the present conflicts in Sudan, Afghanistan, Iraq and Gaza, peace would be achieved much more readily. They would express the suffering that occurs to all non-combatants in war and violence, and would be certain to have a moderating effect.

Chinese philosophy identifies the Yin and Yang—the gentle, caring (female) aspect of nature, and the aggressive, producing (male) aspect.[5] If women are less materially productive, this is a Brownie point for them—they are not promoting the technology spiral. Women and female animals have probably always been more conservative than men and male animals, because they know (mainly from genetic experience) that change makes the rearing of children more difficult in one way or another.

The vital need of young children for their parents

Much has been written about the dual influence of hereditary and environment in determining the characteristics of an individual. Environment is usually regarded in a general way as the physical and social surroundings, the person's interaction with non-living and living things around her/him. What tends to be forgotten is the tremendous importance of the early, formative environment, the child's relationship with its parents. In this permissive era it is convenient to have such a lapse of memory. Yet while a clear advantage is conferred by a happy family to the child's training for a happy and well-adjusted life in the community, its absence leads to the development of violent behaviour and mental disease. (It is not done in western society today to attribute severe psychosis such as schizophrenia to an unhappy relationship with parents in early childhood— since it is wrong to blame anybody for anything—and even medical journals have a reluctance to publish findings of that kind; yet earlier in the twentieth century a considerable body of evidence pointed to such early maladjustment. Nowadays genes take the blame when necessary.) People do not realize how hugely important a secure emotional environment is to children, nor the devastating effects its neglect has on societies.

The mother-child bond

Melvin Konner discusses the imprinting of a mother on to her new-born child, whether animal or human. "... the early experience of attachment, however inappropriate, makes an indelible impression on the brain systems responsible for affection and affiliation, producing tendencies that surface again at a much later, adaptively crucial moment." He describes the soul-searing rhesus monkey experiment done by Harry Harlow

EVOLUTION AND THE NATURE OF GOOD

with surrogate non-living mothers. The infants became deeply attached to the surrogate, clinging the more tightly if it caused them discomfort such as a blast of cold air. Later in life they were socially inept and tended to become autistic. They became sexually incompetent, and if they did have infants, were negligent or brutal towards them.[6] Infant monkeys and apes that do not receive something like hugging and grooming, even though their physical needs are properly attended to, grow up to be socially, emotionally and sexually incompetent.[7]

There is evidence in humans that immediate contact between mother and child after birth is important in moulding the mother's *attitude*. Marshall Klaus and John Kennell found in the early 1980s that measures which improved the survival prospects of premature babies while separating them from their mothers at birth meant that these infants were far more likely than full-term, normal infants to return to hospital as victims of baby battering or neglect. It was as if the long separation of the baby from its mother while it was in intensive care in an incubator had prevented the normal instinctive bond between mother and child from forming at birth, and by the time babies were united with their mothers it was too late for the bond to form.[8]

D. W. Winnicott believes that the earliest contacts between infant and mother are the most vital in ensuring a child's normal emotional development. "... development depends on a good-enough environment, and the earlier we go back in our study of the baby, the more true it is that without good-enough mothering the early stages of [emotional] development cannot take place."[9]

THE ORIGINS OF CO-OPERATION

The severe emotional damage done to children by maternal deprivation (separation or alienation from the mother), its connection with antisocial and criminal behaviour later in life, and its passage from generation to generation due to the incapacity of deprived children to become adequate parents, were studied in detail by John Bowlby and described in his book *Child Care and the Growth of Love* published in 1953.[10] The problem was highlighted by the evacuation of children during the second world war, and the book was preceded in 1951 by Bowlby's report to the World Health Organization entitled *Maternal care and Mental Health.*[11] In spite of the passage of time Bowlby's conclusions are accepted and remain valid today, and the problems he reveals have become more and more acute with the increasing disruption of society.

What he believes to be essential for mental health is that the infant and young child should experience a warm, intimate, and continuous relationship with its mother (or permanent mother-substitute—one person who steadily "mothers" it) in which both find satisfaction and enjoyment. Such a relationship underlies the development of character and mental health. However,"... deprivation will be relatively mild if he has to be looked after by someone whom he has already learned to know and trust..."[12] There are many other ways, besides separation or outright rejection, in which parent-child relationships may become unhealthy: (a) an unconsciously rejecting maternal attitude underlying a loving one; (b) an excessive demand for love and reassurance on the part of a mother; (c) a mother's unconsciously getting satisfaction from a child's behaviour, whilst she thinks she is blaming it.[13] Bowlby adds: "It is only when nature's gifts are lacking that science must study what they are in order to make the best shift it can to replace them.... the normal mother can afford to rely on the prompting of her instincts in the happy knowledge that the tenderness they prompt is what the baby wants."[14]

Below 3 years is the most vulnerable time. Impairment, when it occurs, is physical, intellectual, emotional and social. Even separation as early as three months is probably damaging, though the baby's reaction at this age is not obvious. Between 3 and 5 years the risk is still serious, though much less so than earlier.[15]

The central feature about older children who were deprived in infancy is their inability to make relationships, and all their other disturbances spring from this.[16] On the origins of aggression, Bowlby writes: "No observation is more common than that of the child separated for a few weeks or months during the second, third or fourth years failing to recognize his mother on reunion." This is related to *refusing* to recognize the mother, and is a manifestation of hostility. This hostile reaction to deprivation is what brings about aggressively bad or delinquent behaviour.[17]

Deprivation also injures the power of abstract thinking. "A ... principle of the theory of learning", says Bowlby, "is that an individual cannot learn a skill unless he has a friendly feeling towards his teacher, and is ready to identify himself with her."[18] Sagan and Druyan note that Nim, a chimp, had 60 different trainers over a 4-year period. He was criticised for failure to learn language at an expected rate. But: "Chimps require close

emotional ties for social tasks ... a loving, one-on-one
environment ... might be needed to teach language skills ..."[19]

Paradoxically, the insecurity induced by maternal deprivation
keeps the child dependent and tied to the mother's apron-strings;
it lacks the confidence to venture forth and test the world. The
establishment of "basic trust" in infancy is necessary for the
growth of independence.[20]

Bowlby sees the mother's attitude to the child as being of
fundamental importance. "... the mother needs to feel an
expansion of her own personality in the personality of her child:
each needs to feel closely identified with the other ... the mother
needs to feel that she belongs to her child, and it is only when
she has the satisfaction of this feeling that it is easy for her to
devote herself to it. The provision of constant attention night
and day, seven days a week and 365 days in the year, is possible
only for a woman who derives profound satisfaction from seeing
her child grow from babyhood, through the many phases of
childhood, to become an independent man or woman, and knows
that it is her care which has made this possible."[21] Winnicott
writes:"... the mother should continue to be alive and available,
available physically and available in the sense of not being
preoccupied with something else."[22]

Children, Bowlby says, are often better off in even quite bad
homes than in institutions. "The attachment of children to
parents who, by all ordinary standards, are very bad is a never-
ceasing source of wonder to those who seek to help them." The
fact is that the parents have nevertheless done a great deal for
the child, who has no-one else to depend on.[23]

EVOLUTION AND THE NATURE OF GOOD

The problem tends to be self-perpetuating: "The difficulty for deprived children to become successful parents is perhaps the most damaging of all the effects of deprivation...".   Bad parenthood is a vicious circle.   Professor James Spence of Newcastle University held that one of the principal purposes of the family is the preservation of the art of parenthood.   Bowlby concludes that "... they grow up to reproduce themselves...[24] Deprived children, whether in their own homes or out of them, are the source of social infection as real and serious as are carriers of diphtheria and typhoid."[25]

In the kibbutz movement, in which children are reared communally, the original Israeli women settlers and their daughters had regressed somewhat towards traditional roles. The daughters now demanded and received a longer period of time each day with their children, time significantly entitled "the hour of love".[26]

Communication between mothers and infants

There is no original sin.   Any maladjustment between parents and children starts with the parents, even if it is caused by physical or intellectual difficulties of the child which make it hard to manage.   For Winnicott, discussing anti-social behaviour by adolescents, "we do need to abandon absolutely the theory that children can be born innately amoral."[27]

Desmond Morris writes of the close relationship that exists between mothers and very young infants.   Babies like rhythmic sound; both left- and right-handed mothers hold the baby on their left side, where they hear the heart-beat.[28] As infants two classes of causes make us cry: physical pain and insecurity. Laughing evolved from crying, and its commencement coincides with the development of maternal recognition. At this stage, figures the child sees are threatening, but when it sees that it is the mother it gives a signal half-way between a cry and a parental-recognition gurgle, which is a laugh.

"An agitated mother cannot avoid signalling her agitation to her new-born infant...[29] Some mothers, when feeling agitated, anxious, or cross with the child, try to conceal their mood by forcing a smile. They hope that the counterfeit face will avoid upsetting the infant, but in reality this trick may do more harm than good." It is almost impossible to fool a baby over questions of maternal mood.[30]

Emotional adjustment and learning

The ill-effects of maternal deprivation on learning capacity have been mentioned above. Konner discusses the link of learning with a happy mother-child relationship, and cites Daniel Stern and John S. Watson, who "have independently explored a region of human mental life in which the joy of learning ... is very nearly joined to the joy of love."[31] The role of the teacher is far from being limited to imparting information, especially with young children. At a course for Zimbabwean Health Assistants, a member was asked how he would teach a class of six-year-old children about hygiene. "Well," he began, "I would lecture—" "If you lecture, and you die, you will go straight down there!"

said the course tutor, pointing at the molten centre of the Earth. "They don't want lectures, they want love!" In teaching children of all ages, rapport between teacher and pupils is essential. Erwin Schrödinger writes: "If only teachers, including parents, would take to heart the necessity of mutual understanding! We cannot exert any lasting influence over those entrusted to us without it."[32]

Child rearing in non-westernised societies

Compared with westernized humans, South African !Kung babies have access to much more interaction with the mother and to much more general physical and social experience. Indulgence by the mother is absolute, including breast feeding at all times (up to some time in the fourth year). The process of separation is initiated by the infant, who passes fairly gradually from an intense attachment to the mother to the receptive context of a group of children, who range in age from near-peers to adolescent caretakers. These become a major focus of the child's social behaviour.[33] Among the !Kung, and also in all "higher" primates, mother and infant sleep in immediate proximity (if not direct physical contact) in the same bed (or nest). The same is true, with little variation, for all non-industrial human societies.[34]

Margaret Mead has pointed out that many studies of multiple-caretaking have failed to show that it has any objectively detectable unfortunate consequences, provided that the two or three or several caretakers offer an adequately nurturant and uninterrupted human environment. Robert LeVine has confirmed this.[35]

Sexual relationships

It is a commonplace that evolutionary success depends on the ability to survive combined with the number of offspring that can be produced. Where the young need a period of care from one or both parents, the latter condition needs to be modified: the number of young surviving depends not only on the number produced, but also on the maintenance of conditions in which they can be reared. In humans, behaviour that keeps parents together has therefore been selected for rather than the ability to produce great numbers of children. Because mothers have a greater role in child care than fathers, females that are careful in selecting mates for their staying-power have a genetic advantage over those who do not discriminate, whereas males gain by mating with a wider range of females. As E.O. Wilson says, in reproduction male animals are put to much less trouble while providing an equal genetic investment. "It pays males to be aggressive, hasty, fickle and undiscriminating. In theory it is more profitable for females to be coy, to hold back until they can identify males with the best genes. In species that rear young, it is also important for the females to select males who are more likely to stay with them after insemination."[36]

EVOLUTION AND THE NATURE OF GOOD

Pairing

Humans are pair-bonding, but imperfectly so. Distant species such as the ringdove have families most similar to ours. Although immediately descended from a promiscuous, non-pairing form of ape, we have re-acquired the family system, which, in an extended form, was a characteristic of our earlier hunting mammal ancestors. We have also re-invented the pair-bond, but it rests less securely on us than on our distant avian cousins.

Marriage was invented by birds, which respect it much more conscientiously than people and have never needed complicated contracts or divorce laws. Mary and John Gribbin tell us that "Monogamy ... is the rule in more than 95% of all known bird species ... this is related to the enormous effort parents have to make to raise their chicks successfully, an effort that requires the full-time attention of both parents... Starting out from a typical mammalian mode of reproduction, human beings have gone a long way down the same path as that taken by birds, and for the same reason: the need for both parents to cooperate in raising the young ...".[37] In lions and many other species, the young must be trained to hunt by their parents.[38] This requires the parents to stay together in extended family groups. Among the primates, gibbons (very differently from our closest relations the chimpanzees) marry for life.[39]

THE ORIGINS OF CO-OPERATION

Family formation

Species such as chimpanzees which do not have pair-bonding ensure protection for their offspring by taking communal responsibility for them. Eugene Marais explains that in baboons, which are promiscuous and have an inherent and insistent desire for change, "male parental affection as it exists among monogamous animals is ... inconceivable ...". However, what males "lack in individual parental affection is quite made up for by a common concern for all the young ones of the troop. It is a potent and real passion." Sometimes they fearlessly and even recklessly risk their lives in the attempt to save a young one.[40] We humans share the need for family formation not only with other large hunting mammals but also with a very varied selection of the animal kingdom. Pair-bonding species include about 8,000 species of birds, as well as marmosets (small South American monkeys), gibbons, and a few members of the dog family such as coyotes and bat-eared foxes. In these species the male tends to contribute substantially to the care of the young.[41] Among birds, one parent cannot rear chicks because the nest has to be guarded. Their strategy rules are these: (1) polygamy is forbidden; (2) copulation with or by an unmated female is pointless, because alone, she cannot look after a nest and rear a family; (3) surreptitious fertilization by one male of another male's mate is a viable strategy. Males also engage in "divorce insurance", courting but not mating with passing females.[42]

EVOLUTION AND THE NATURE OF GOOD

Marriage among hunter-gatherers

Konner discusses marriage among the South African !Kung group of hunter-gatherers. Marriage "is arranged, as it has been in most human societies throughout most of history."[43] We are inclined to think of arranged marriages, holding together people who are not naturally attracted to each other, as an invention of modern societies. However, those primitive communities, in which the man had the separate role of breadwinner (hunter), may have found arranged marriages necessary, to ensure that the parents of a child stay together and look after it. The !Kung frequently divorce from these early marriages, although they rarely do so once a child has been born to them.[44]

Sexual predispositions from our animal and hominid ancestry

Our pre-primate ancestors were hunters, and so, like modern lions, had to form extended family groups in which the males provided food and protected the young. Our later primate forbears, however, abandoned hunting and so lost the family system.

Jared Diamond traces the subsequent evolution of human sexuality. From the vegetarian diet of our ape ancestors, we diverged within the last several million years to become once again social carnivores as well. To hunt we had to use brains; as a result, human children took years to acquire all the information and practice needed. Chimp fathers offer protection on a communal basis, but chimps do not form pair-bonds. The chimp system, in which several adult males are likely to copulate with the same oestrous female, would not work for us. The human father, who will contribute much to the care of the child, must know it is his. This becomes a need because there are other men around—we live in close social groups, originally necessitated by hunting and gathering. Our societies, like our food habits, resemble those of lions and wolves: we live in bands containing many adult males and many adult females. But unlike them, because our children need prolonged rearing, we pair off, in which respect we resemble colonies of seabirds like gulls and penguins.[45]

Kin obligation

Kin selection

Kin selection is a biological process in which the genes of animals which help their relatives are more likely to survive than the genes of those which do not, since many genes are common to relatives. The result is that animals have an inherent contract with their closest relatives. It arises from the operation of kin selection in the past, which has enabled their mutual survival. If they honour this contract they will continue to survive together; such a contract is biologically sound.

EVOLUTION AND THE NATURE OF GOOD

Obligation to near relatives

Jane Goodall describes the way that chimpanzees help their kin—the closer, the more actively.[46]

Like other animals, we humans have inherited an obligation to help people more distantly related to us than our children and not in the immediate line of descent, such as siblings, nieces and nephews, and cousins. Our sympathy, or empathy, is strongly biased in favour of close kin.[47] Closeness of kin is measurable in simple genetic terms. For instance, 50% of DNA allelomorphs are shared by parents and children, 50% by sibs, 25% are shared with grandparents and with blood aunts and uncles, and 12.5% with cousins. The lesson of kin selection for us is that just as it is right for us to look after our children to promote their welfare and continue the survival of our species, so to a lesser extent do we have an obligation to less closely related family members. All humans, says Peter Singer, have "obligations on members of a family to support their kin and constraints on sexual relationships... the significance of these universals lies in the fact that [such] obligations form the core of all human ethical systems—and they also guide the behaviour of our close non-human relatives."[48]

Nature thus imposes on us an obligation towards kin and others connected with us—the closer, the greater the obligation.

THE ORIGINS OF CO-OPERATION

Altruism

Kin selection is mediated by altruism, or action which benefits others at the expense of oneself. It is found in species very remote from ourselves and does not depend on the complexity of the species.[50] Edward O. Wilson points to the altruism of the highly social insects, ants, bees and wasps. In the case of social insects especially, he says, natural selection has been broadened to include kin selection. Human altruism varies from that of the soldier throwing himself on a hand grenade to protect his fellows to a dozen minor acts of self-sacrifice that parents will do for their children every day. Although the form and intensity of human altruistic acts are to a large extent culturally determined, the underlying motivation evolves through genes.[51]

Wilson attacks altruism as related to nepotism, and as "the enemy of civilization", because it would never lead to international cooperation.[52] His remarks could be interpreted, however, as meaning that when—as often happens nowadays—we are compelled to negotiate in great groups, such as corporations, social classes and nations, co-operation for mutual benefit, and not kin obligation, is the only effective basis for interaction.

Obligation to the community and the human race as a whole

Co-operation, as well as kinship, is important in determining an ethical code. As Midgley says, "We are beings that naturally care directly for others, as well as for ourselves."[49] We thus have

EVOLUTION AND THE NATURE OF GOOD

a heavy obligation to those on whom we depend for cooperation, the outstanding example being the spouse whose children we share. Socialized groups of animals, including humans, develop a need for reciprocation and co-operation on many fronts. The principle is: "You scratch my back and I'll scratch yours."

To a lesser extent, and for the same reason, we extend a measure of beneficence to our immediate circle and to all humans, the species with whose members we are able to reproduce and so share genes. There is a fundamental unity among human beings. They are amply able to feel sympathy for non-kin. There is a common thread of moral standards among humans though they differ in their codes because of their different cultures.[53] Tending the sick, for example, has been an important part of human behaviour since long before the rise of our modern civilization. The Neanderthals took care of their sick and aged.[54] In considering how much of our harmful cultural baggage we can dispense with, it is encouraging to know that simple care and kindness are so deep-rooted, and that we would not lose them if we were to abandon technology and the trappings of civilization.

Co-operation with all other living things

We have developed close relations with some animals, including dogs, cats, horses and farm animals, and have acquired an obligation to look after them. But beyond this, it has become very clear lately that the whole of the animal and vegetable kingdoms form a vast, inter-connected and hitherto stable ecosphere, and we fail to care for it very much at our peril.

Chapter 5
Mutual help is indispensable to humans

People are absolutely dependent on each other. The idea of anyone surviving alone cannot be entertained. A review of our evolutionary history makes this clear; the welfare of one entails the welfare of all. We are wholly dependent on the system by which people interact to mutual benefit. The culture of sharing is the only one that enables survival.[1] Relations between people are fundamental in this; they are not merely one of the things that enable humans to survive. We have become totally dependent on intra-species co-operation.

The need of all animals for mutual help

Petr Kropotkin (1902) and Robert Trivers (1971) both said that animals assist each other precisely because by doing so they achieve long term, collective benefits of greater value than the short term benefits derived from straightforward competition.[2] This includes: (a) simple bilateral co-operation, (b) more widespread generosity in the expectation of reciprocity based on reputation, and (c) true uncalculated altruism.[3]

EVOLUTION AND THE NATURE OF GOOD

Socialization in animals and *Homo*

I have discussed socialization in a previous book.[4] It is the development, through evolution, of co-operation between individuals because of mutual interest. It is experienced subjectively as compassion or fellow-feeling. It is essentially an instinctive and emotional attribute of animals and humans, not the product of rational thought. It has been passed on by evolution over the ages and is not dependent on culture, which is the handing-down of acquired knowledge from one generation to the next.

The earliest and most deeply-ingrained manifestations of socialization are motherhood, sex and fatherhood, perhaps in that order. In primates, sex is for much more than reproduction. It serves as a mechanism of socialization; this is clearest among the bonobos.[5] Once the family nucleus has been formed, animals start to look to neighbouring members of their species for cooperation to increase their security further.

Socialization, or in that sense civilization, is by no means confined to humans; indeed we often fall short of the standards set by other animals. Monkeys, apes and other wild beasts, say Carl Sagan and Ann Druyan, are powerfully inhibited against shedding blood within the group. "... we under-value our non-human ancestors when we blame them for our violent proclivities. Very likely, they had inhibitions in place that we routinely circumvent."[6] The authors note that "Cooperation, friendship and altruism are ... chimp traits" and recall "the macaques who would rather go hungry than administer an electric shock to other, not closely related macaques—going so far as to reject even substantial incentives."[7]

The extent of socialization beyond the immediate family varies greatly between closely-related species and even within one species, depending upon the environment to which the group is normally subjected. Melvin Konner tells us that "Variation in social structure within one species in different environments can be as great as variation across the whole primate order." We cannot extrapolate the social organization of, for instance, our hominid ancestors from our own.[8] "The species-specific, 'hard-wired' equipment includes if-then statements ... for behaviour."[9] On a scale of social structure complexity among primates, "... Japanese monkeys clearly are closest to humans, followed by baboons; while chimpanzees, our nearest relatives, appear rather disorderly; and orangutans, also close cousins of ours, have no social structure at all—just a mother with offspring and an occasional male visitor."[10]

Jean Jacques Rousseau believed co-operation, pity and altruism to be natural to *Homo*.[11] Charles Darwin, pondering the meaning of life for one who does not believe in God or Heaven, believed such a one would find "in accordance with the verdict of all the wisest men that the highest satisfaction is derived from following certain impulses, namely the social instincts. If he acts for the good of others, he will receive the approbation of his fellow men and gain the love of those with whom he lives; and this latter gain is undoubtedly the highest pleasure on this earth."[12]

EVOLUTION AND THE NATURE OF GOOD

One result of this innate spirit of mutual concern is that we do not and cannot harm one or more people to help others. If we were able to save ten children by throwing one to the lions, we would not do it. At a more realistic level, we cannot use a utilitarian approach to such things as drug trials and the use of vaccines; possible injury to one healthy person precludes it.

Peter Singer brings out the failure of self-interest to make people happy. "... genuine indifference to ethics of any sort is rare[13]... Today the assertion that life is meaningless no longer comes from existentialist philosophers who treat it as a shocking discovery; it comes from bored adolescents, to whom it is a truism. Perhaps it is the central place of self-interest, and the way in which we conceive of our own interest, that is to blame here... Such a life is often a self-defeating enterprise. The ancients knew of the 'paradox of hedonism', according to which the more explicitly we pursue our desire for pleasure, the more elusive we will find its satisfaction[14]...

"The individual pursuit of self-interest can be collectively self-defeating." Singer gives the example of using a car instead of public transport.[15]

The development of culture

Culture is not by any means the exclusive province of humans. It has developed in tandem with the mammalian brain. It is, in essence, the ability to pass on learned behaviour to offspring, and it enables a species to adapt to a changing environment much more quickly than by genetic change, or "the survival of the fittest". (As I have pointed out in a previous book, cultural advance compromises the survival of the fittest, and contains the seeds of species extinction.[16])

Though we are inclined to think of culture as a civilizing influence, it is not in fact the source of our co-operation and need for mutual help. That is innate and is a legacy from our early animal ancestors.

Chimpanzees make much use of cultural learning. Although they have used it to adopt a dominance hierarchy, chimp life is far from being a military parade. Frans de Waal wrote: "The law of the jungle does not apply to chimpanzees. Their network of coalitions limits the right of the strongest; everybody pulls strings."[17]

Political organization in animals and *Homo*

In animals, strict dominance relationships are often an effective means by which conflicts can be negotiated. Dominant members can enforce *conflict intervention* and *protective intervention*. Tonkean macaques, however, are an advancedly democratic species. These functions devolve to "lower" individuals as the society becomes more democratic. There may then be *mediation*. There is also *celebration* after a major conflict has been resolved.[18]

Thomas Hobbes wrote that there has to be organized government to keep order.[19] Hobbes also appears to suggest that totalitarian government is the most effective. We may trace the development of different forms of government from its origins in early communities. Robert

EVOLUTION AND THE NATURE OF GOOD

Ardrey places the number of hunters required by hominid and early human bands at about 11—this number, he reminds us, is seen in many social, management and sporting contexts in modern life, and is why workers function best in small groups. This fixed the size of a community at about 50. It was important for everybody to know everyone else, so that that the group could make full use of the potential available.[20] Mark Nathan Cohen describes how the "band societies" of pre-agricultural humans minimize their formal politics. Group decisions are commonly made by consensus, and leadership is rarely if ever reinforced by coercive power. Bands are typically small, informal networks of friends and kin who know each other personally, who deal with each other as individuals and as friends and relatives, and who remain together largely because of mutual dependence and positive feelings toward one another. Economic exchange, or reciprocity, usually takes place informally, on the basis of need, social obligation, and personal ties—rather than on the basis of market value and profit. Such societies are not "egalitarian" to all of their members.[21] In hunter-gatherer societies, each individual was acknowledged and given appropriate recognition by the others, each had a place and a function in the community, and each had the right to call on the others for help when necessary. Decisions affecting the whole group were reached by consensus at a meeting attended by everybody or by family heads. Even today, this community spirit persists in small villages and rural communities throughout the world. When many

MUTUAL HELP IS INDISPENSABLE TO HUMANS

Shetlanders became snowbound by the severe weather of December 1995, the newspapers reported that their situation was much relieved because they were accustomed to helping each other. In Swaziland, a predominantly rural society, it is usual for people of all races to greet strangers of any race as they pass in the street. In great cities such as London it is almost comical to observe how people avoid each other. A high proportion of residents do not know their next-door neighbours. One theory of broadsheet newspapers is that they have been designed this way to prevent conversation on tube-trains. Everybody is much too close, and we have an in-built drive to keep a space round us.

As Garrett Hardin points out, the hunter-gatherer social system—which is really communism of the type proposed by Marx—does not work when numbers grow larger and individual performance cannot be monitored by neighbours who know and have social connections with the person, and can exert peer pressure: people as a large group will only put effort into their contribution to society if they reap a reward as a result of the effort.[22] In nations, communism has to be imposed by a dictator or oligarchy, and the leadership, itself subject to similar human failings, may become corrupt. Jesus adopted communism for his twelve disciples, a number very close to Ardrey's ideal of 11 for co-operating workers.

In summary, small groups of humans or other animals, where everybody knows everybody else, can co-operate without a formal political system. As human groups grow larger, control can only be achieved by developing a dominance hierarchy.

EVOLUTION AND THE NATURE OF GOOD

With the advance of culture, technology and acquisitiveness, however, the alpha members come to abuse their authority; the other members of the community, whose culture and political awareness have likewise advanced, revolt against the oppression and the system no longer works. Democracy has been evolved as a result, but it is indeed a tender flower, requiring a population that not only is culturally advanced and educated, but retains a strong sense of duty towards others. Because of its fragile nature, democracy often breaks down in the modern world, and the great resources and technological tools available to the tyrant or oligarchy that emerges mean that he or they can cause enormous suffering to the people. Such a situation has arisen at the time of writing in Zimbabwe.

The way we relate to each other

Although culture plays a part in the expression of moral drives, they are based on sympathy. We relate to people and do not, in the first instance, calculate our dealings with them.

In an earlier book I have discussed the nature of truth.[23] It is not absolute but is perceived differently by each individual. Our view is subjective, and is formed not only by our peculiar anatomy but, deeper than that, by the experiences of our ancestors. We cannot, therefore, derive an absolute universal truth to apply to the whole world, but each has his/her own separate truth. Consequently, relationships between people are not defined by logically derived *facts* based on universal truth. They are governed by *attitudes* between people.

MUTUAL HELP IS INDISPENSABLE TO HUMANS

We are innately socialized, and our evolutionary history tells us that a social and charitable attitude towards each other is right and will be successful. It is not effective to work out who is right and who is wrong; rightness and wrongness are differently assessed by different people. The effective and successful way to relate to people is by being charitable and expecting the best, especially in the first instance. Christianity and the other main religions teach one to work on this basis. Other animals do the same—they take an attitude to one another, and primarily it is an attitude of cooperation. The much-researched "tit-for-tat" strategy—being charitable in the first instance, and then responding the same way as the other party—has been shown experimentally to be the most successful in achieving co-operation. So charity, as advocated by the religious, is right. To achieve it one has to undo much of the institutional selfishness built into the western way of life: profit from shares, exploitation of the Third World, etc.

The world is full of people who want to deal with each other in a fair and just, or even generous, manner; not only those with whom they have close kinship or work together closely, but all people with whom they have contact. It is also full of people who have an intrinsic drive to honour contracts of all kinds, and who feel uncomfortable and unhappy if they fail to do so. Such contracts are not only written or legal ones, but include all the informal understandings that exist between people, from the small-scale dealings and unspoken assents of our everyday lives to the all-embracing social contract written about by Robert Ardrey.[24] We forget how pervasive are these attitudes, which have for the vast majority of human history been the cement of our society. Only with the growth of warring tribes, cities, leaders, great feudal landowners, industry and capital, have we by degrees been brainwashed into the great fallacy of modern democracy, thinking that rivalry for money and power, under the guiding hand of the State, is the right and natural way of life for humans. Although that is the way most people behave now, it is not in our genes, which are virtually the same as those of our hunter-gatherer ancestors.

The close relationship of all humans

The recent common origin of present-day humans

Humans are much more closely related to each other than most species. The evidence for this is reviewed in my book *Evolution and the Spiral of Technology*.[25] Chris Stringer writes that "*Homo sapiens*, far from being a disparate group of races and populations, is fundamentally homogeneous; we are so young a species that we have not had time to differentiate in any meaningful way."[26] Jared Diamond points out that "Two million years ago, several proto-human lineages had coexisted side by side until a shake-up left only one [*Homo erectus* in Africa]. It now appears that a similar shake-up occurred within the last 60,000 years, and that all of us alive in the world today are descended from the winner of that upheaval."[27] Stringer supports this close relationship with evidence from studies of mitochondrial DNA, which is transmitted only through the female line. The mitochondrial DNA of Eskimos and

MUTUAL HELP IS INDISPENSABLE TO HUMANS

Australian aborigines is more similar than that of two groups of African lowland gorillas that may encounter each other in the forest. Chimp and orang-utan mitochondrial DNA has also revealed both of these species to be considerably more diverse than *Homo sapiens sapiens.* "Mankind has only recently evolved from one tight little group of ancestors," says Stringer. The common ancestor, or small group of ancestors, who gave rise to our close mitochondrial DNA lineage must have lived about 200,000 years ago. Based on mitochondrial DNA, Merriwether *et al.* found that "the native African populations have the greatest diversity and, consistent with evidence from a variety of sources, [the study] suggests an African origin for our species." From studies of nuclear DNA, Kidd *et al.* found that Africa shows marked variability, while the rest of the world does not. Because those who set off from their African home to conquer the world were made up of a tribe or group of African *Homo sapiens* who possessed a very limited pattern, they must have been a small and limited group.[28]

There is thus a close genetic relationship between all present-day humans, and, indeed, between ourselves and our ancestors back to Cro-Magnon times (35,000 years ago) or earlier. The Cro-Magnons are greatly admired for their art. Erich Harth thinks it likely that palaeolithic man was genetically equipped to live in the 20th century, if exposed throughout life to its culture.[29] New-Guineans have learned modern technology, from their Stone Age, in one generation; Cro-Magnons could probably have done the same.[30]

EVOLUTION AND THE NATURE OF GOOD

Racial differences are superficial

When people stay in the same place for a few generations they develop a superficial similarity. Such a grouping is dubbed a "race". Underneath they are very like other "races", and individual diversity is the main variation.[31] Richard Lewontin found that there is more genetic variation within one race than there is between that race and another.[32] Within Africa people have been moving away from each other and forming separate groups longer than elsewhere, so although they are all called "blacks" they are more diverse than all the people in the other continents. Human mobility has led to much mixing of peoples, which further increases the similarity between the different groups which we now regard as races. The superficial differences, such as variously coloured skin and variously shaped noses and skulls, caused by races' diverse environments are very obvious; that is why we tend to see large differences between races.[33]

Because of their close relationship, present-day human races all have very similar brains and a very similar intellectual potential. Success means correct adaptation to the circumstances in which they live, leading to a stable existence. Bearing this in mind, it is entirely wrong to say that western types of *Homo* are greater achievers, or better-adjusted; indeed, the accelerating change and frenetic activity in the lives of westernized peoples indicates that this is the reverse of the truth. A former governor of Kenya wrote in the 1950s that the British colonies in

MUTUAL HELP IS INDISPENSABLE TO HUMANS

Africa were "populated by people who had never invented or adopted an alphabet or even any form of hieroglyphic writing... They had no numerals, no almanac or calendar, no notation of time or measurements of length, capacity or weight, no currency, no external trade except slaves and ivory... no plough, no wheel and no means of transportation except human head porterage on land and dugout canoes on rivers and lakes. These people had built nothing, nothing of any kind, in any material more durable than mud, poles and thatch. Great numbers wore no clothes at all; others wore bark cloth or hides and skins."[34] These remarks, evidently intended to be highly critical of the people for whom he held responsibility, are really a description of how they are better adjusted than the governor's own society.

To humans "good" can only be the good of humans and other living things

When we come to decide what good consists of, our opinion is determined by our evolutionary history. Ethics is about our relations with other people and animals. In thinking of doing good, we cannot relate it to anything except our treatment of others, whether close kin, other humans, other animals or, at the greatest stretch, all living things including plants. We have evolved to think of good in this way, and are intrinsically incapable of any other idea of good. Religions which have conceived other kinds of good have done so by introducing supernatural beings who compete with our fellow-humans for

EVOLUTION AND THE NATURE OF GOOD

our favours. Thomas Hobbes wrote that nothing can be unjust (immoral) unless it is relation to other people.[35] David Hume recognized that humanity is innate in people and found it to be the source of morality.[36] For Thomas Nagle, "There is no substitute for a direct concern for other people as the basis of morality."[37]

Chapter 6
Help to others should be graded according to kinship and obligation

Contracts are the basis of ethical behaviour

Ethical behaviour among socialized beings takes the form of contracts, rather than a diffuse obligation to all as seen by the utilitarians. Having evolved in the way that they have, animals can only fulfil their ethical obligations by means of contracts. The original contracts are innate, inherited and instinctive, and are between immediate or remote kin, varying in degree of obligation according to closeness to each other. As animals have become increasingly dependent on other members of their species, contracts have also developed between those, not necessarily related, who co-operate with each other. The effect of cultural development has been merely to refine methods of co-operation—and later, to abuse them. Our primary moral failure is a failure to honour contracts.

John Rawls traces the theory of the social contract to Locke, Rousseau and Kant. The guiding idea is that justice in the basic structure of society is created by the original agreement, not by various man-made codes. "The principles of justice are chosen behind a veil of ignorance... it seems that the principle of utility is incompatible with the conception of social cooperation among equals for mutual advantage."[1]   In discussing the question of rights, Mary Midgley says the "'rights of man' ... were not supposed to be ones conferred by law, since the whole point of appealing to them was to change laws so as to embody them." Midgley inveighs against the exclusion of compassion from the consideration of moral behaviour.[2]

Many of the writers in Peter Singer's anthology *Ethics*[3] regard the social contract simply as a market-type arrangement between people. But in Robert Ardrey's book *The Social Contract*, he sees the contract as entirely based on human evolutionary history and as the result of deeply-embedded instincts.[4]

The biological origin of contracts

The forming of contracts occurs in many species both pre-mammalian and mammalian.   It seems clear that ethics should be based on a contractual system, unless we aim to behave contrary to Nature.

Contracts and utilitarianism

A conflict will inevitably arise between our general obligation to the environment and to humanity in general, and our particular obligation to those close to us by kinship or common interest.

HELP TO OTHERS SHOULD BE GRADED

The use of an antibiotic for an unpleasant but not fatal or permanently disabling illness, for instance, will cut it short, but may contribute to the increasing prevalence of drug resistance in the community.

Jean Jacques Rousseau, writing in 1762, as well as Robert Ardrey in recent times, both used the title "The Social Contract" for their` books on human relationships; in this way they emphasised the importance of contracts in our lives rather than a diffuse obligation to the whole of mankind. As we have seen, the contracts are with our closest kin, and with those with whom we cooperate most closely for mutual benefit.

For Mary Warnock, "...to concentrate too much on the width rather than the depth of our human sympathies may lead not only to absurdly impossible duties, but to the neglect of duties which we can and must fulfil, which are truly binding, and which are nearer home... we should distinguish between sympathy and a kind of universal benevolence or beneficence."[5]

Opposing the extreme utilitarian view, Singer quotes the example of a surgeon who can save two lives by forfeiting one which would otherwise have survived, and asks: would researchers be prepared to carry out a potentially lethal experiment on a human orphan under six months old if that were the only way to save thousands of lives? Singer's point illustrates an important principle of ethics. It is wrong for a few to be harmed in order to benefit many. Such action, which can only take place as a product of cultural development, cuts across the social contract and the means by which our species has learned to live together. To take an example which exercised the medical profession in recent years, if a whooping cough vaccine which can be expected to prevent the disease and save a number of lives produces serious reactions in some of its recipients, it cannot be used. Singer sums this up as Rules versus Values: "... it makes sense to maximise a value—to increase it as much as possible—whereas we can only comply with a rule. So if I value happiness, I can choose between acts that will lead to there being more or less happiness in the world, but if I accept the rule that one should never kill an innocent human being, I can only comply with this rule, or break it."[6] In other words, we must stick to the rules and honour our contracts; this is different from seeking universal good or universal happiness. It implies a fading of our obligations to others in proportion to their remoteness from us. Happiness is a very complex thing, including relationships with others and concern for *their* happiness. It would be impossible to *work out* what actions result in the greatest universal happiness. We have to live according to principles based on our instinct to co-operate, and on our sliding-scale contracts with kin and other humans and animals.

The tragedy of the commons

Garrett Hardin writes that "At one extreme of the spectrum of discriminating altruisms lies *universalism*, altruism that is practised without discrimination of kinship, shared values, acquaintanceship, propinquity in time or space, or any other characteristic. An immense literature has grown up

promoting [this] ideal ..." Universalism, says Hardin,
"promotes a pathology ... namely the tragedy of the
commons." By this Hardin means that if a group of people,
not closely knit by ties of family or friendship, share a
common service, they will take all they can from it and not
ensure that the service is maintained in a fit state for all users.
The "commons", for instance, may be a field shared for the
grazing of cattle; users will let their own animals take all the
grass they can, and no-one will limit grazing so that the field
remains productive. In short, action is divorced from
consequences. "The more impersonal the relationship", says
Hardin, "the greater the probability of cheating."[7] He quotes
Adam Smith, who said in 1759: "The administration of the
great system of the universe ... the care of the universal
happiness of all rational and sensible beings, is the business
of God, and not of man. To man is allotted a much humbler
department, but one much more suitable to the weakness of
his powers, and to the narrowness of his comprehension—the
care of his own happiness, of that of his family, his friends,
his country."[8]

Grading of contractual obligation

If we accept that contracts, and not a diffuse effort to achieve
universal happiness, are the right guide to conduct, it follows
that our obligation to others has to be graded; we owe more care
to some than to others.

EVOLUTION AND THE NATURE OF GOOD

We have some obligation to all living things

In Midgley's view, considering animals as excluded from our moral behaviour is one result of a neglect of compassion and humanity. "The doubtful credit for confining justice to the human species seems to belong to Grotius, who finally managed to ditch the Roman notion of *jus naturale*, natural right or law, common to all species."[9]

Singer, to whom the prevention of suffering is the predominant need, actually claims that animals deserve equal consideration to humans from us.[10] Yet by the same token, he argues against deep ecology because non-sentient beings such as plants need no consideration.[11] This argument, however, is faulty because the integrity of the biosphere is necessary to *all* its inhabitants; therefore it should be maintained in the interests of humans and of all our near and far living relations, and we need to include plants, even if remotely, among the objects of our care.

Grading of obligation is necessary

Our co-operation is not uniform with all living things, all animals species, or even for all people. The mode of our evolution dictates that our obligation to others depends on the degree of our kinship with them, and on the extent to which we co-operate with them. Among the latter, the outstanding one is the other parent of our children. Our concern for other living things will inevitably vary according to the closeness of our kinship or mutual obligation with them.

Edward Westermarck notes that affection of parents, including fathers, for children is universal, and this includes those in totally "undeveloped" communities. Sibs and more distant relatives show tapering obligations. He also suggests that primitive people extend a sense of obligation more widely than developed peoples.[12]

James Rachels writes that "'Kin altruism', as it is called, leads individuals to care for their relatives just to the extent that those relatives share the individual's genes. This explains why we are especially concerned for the welfare of our children and siblings, somewhat less for our cousins (who share fewer of our genes), and even less for strangers."[13]   (The reason for our heavy obligation to co-parents, even though they do not share more of our alleles than the general population, is because if we did not honour it, our offspring would tend to die off.)

The obligation of non-intervention

In some ways our obligation towards other humans can be seen to extend much further out than the circle in which we participate—it then becomes an obligation of non-intervention. A.C. Ewing writes "It is felt that people should not be regarded ... merely as receptacles into which to pour as much good as possible but as being in special individual relations to the agent."[14]

EVOLUTION AND THE NATURE OF GOOD

Harm done by violating this obligation of non-intervention

Attempts to recognize and fulfil obligations to the whole world equally, not driven by emotion and spontaneous motivation, can lead to bad consequences. Sometimes we try to apply mass measures without feeling because they save or prolong life, or because it has always been done, or because the livelihood of the doer depends on the doing. Efforts to extend help too widely often result in abuse, the misdirection of aid and the disruption of the life of those being helped. While our first duty is towards kin and those with whom we cooperate, our second duty is inaction towards those more remote and for whom we have no particular feeling, until we have closely examined our motivations. Activity in relation to them, which is now possible because of technology, often results in damage—and is often motivated by greed. These activities are clearly related to the utilitarian ethic. On the break-up of the Soviet Union huge pressure came on the Russians and those of other member countries to change their way of life, not merely by removing the tyranny to which they had been subjected, but also by abandoning socialism and adopting a capitalist economy. This was fostered largely by the economic interests of westerners, and promoted with enthusiasm by the economic entrepreneurs in the ex-Soviet Union countries themselves. The people were torn from their long-established life-style, and many were not able to be competitive and suffered severely in the new economic conditions. On a western assessment the people of China have been tyrannised. Government has been handed down from emperors, and most recently from the communist state. Because the communist doctrine threatened western democracies, it became a credo of the west to bring down the communist government and introduce a democratic system. As this process develops, the age-old rural lifestyle of the great majority, with its stability and in-built moral standards, has been eroded away, with severely unsettling effects on the youth of those communities. It has seemed to the average westerner that democracy and western ideas of human rights must be introduced, but the effect is very destructive. Colonial, missionary, and economic expansion in Africa and Asia was a violation of the obligation of the non-intervention rule which had disastrous consequences for the people of those continents.

To attempt to extend the contract too far afield may be hazardous, for the following reasons:

(1) Those closer to us may be neglected; an example is the devoted charity supporter who finds her work more important than her family.

(2) Damage may be done by giving material aid where it might be more helpful to leave (or assist) the group to make its own adjustment, by learning to solve its own problems.

(3) Lack of knowledge of, and of rapport with, groups considerably different from one's own means that one's assessment of their needs may be wrong.

(4) The determining of needs is very subjective. It has been a common assumption that what the Third World requires is a western way of life; part of my previous book has been devoted to showing that this view is disastrously in error.[15]

(5) Giving help without the urge to help may lead to hypocrisy, cynicism and self-serving.

Conversely, one should not impose obligation to oneself

Practical ethics includes not making demands on others, for instance expecting care when one is old. In general, it is a good thing for people to manage by themselves and it is right to aim at this.

The obligation to repair damage done by wrong intervention

These considerations do not, however, detract from the culturally-acquired obligation which developed nations now have to mitigate the ill-effects that their technology has had on third-world communities. Ethics is much complicated by human culture, as will be seen in Part IV.

An example of obligation and of appropriate help is where people have left their homes to work in a wholly different environment, perhaps urban instead of rural. It becomes the duty of the employer to recognize the obligation thereby imposed by the social contract and ensure that all the employees' needs are met. Another example of such obligation is that which the colonial nations have acquired to the countries whose societies and economies they have disrupted; they have the duty of assisting them, in a more enlightened way, through the resulting crisis. Such enlightenment must include ceasing to export western industrial practices which upset ordinary

HELP TO OTHERS SHOULD BE GRADED

people's way of life, ceasing to create conditions that cause huge debts to accrue, ceasing to sell arms; and—as Hardin suggests—placing population control before death control.[16] An example of inappropriate help is extending a grant or a soft loan to a developing country to build dams or factories which disrupt people' accustomed way of life, or to develop for commercial purposes land which is required for peasant farming. Such projects often have strings attached which will benefit the donor country.

PART III
MORALITY AS DICTATED BY HUMAN EVOLUTION

Chapter 7
The development of ethics in our ancestors

Ancient origins of ethics

What is right? If it is indeed the welfare of humans, it is logical to look at the features of life that were keeping *Homo* surviving and stable before the onset of our headlong culture.

"Since Darwin," writes Peter Singer, "there has been a widely supported scientific theory that offers an explanation of the origin of ethics.[1]... As long as we remain on the level of the explanation of ethics, rather than the justification of a particular view about what we ought to do, evolutionary theory has an important role to play in helping us to understand the characteristics common to primate ethics, and why ethics exists at all."[2] Natural attitudes are benevolent, and it is in a natural frame of mind that we can approach our duties to others.

ANCESTRAL DEVELOPMENT OF ETHICS

There is nothing magical about good behaviour. It is the same for humans as for animals. And therefore it is right to seek the only formula for an ethical code in our ancestry and our evolution. Every ethical system has originated in the human mind, a biological entity. There are no absolute moral truths out there waiting to be discovered. We are bound to our empirical existence, and our moral sense is therefore grounded firmly in the human world.[3] We must look to our social instincts for proper behaviour, because we have evolved to depend completely for our survival on co-operation with other people. Joseph Needham wrote: "The evolutionary process itself supplies us with a criterion of the good."[4]

Right behaviour depends on the biological needs of oneself and others, and can be thought of as that course of action that will lead us and our species to a graceful and smooth end in due time. What we think instinctively is right or should be done is guidance from our genes—it is the result of the experience of our forbears. It should not therefore be ignored. For instance, as time has gone on we have developed empathy with animals. If the idea of an animal getting injured hurts us, it is because it is now in our interests to make common cause with that species of animal. According to Mary and John Gribbin, "Ethics, moral codes and the teachings of the great religions are powerful forces in human affairs because they are right, not in any subjective sense but in the sense that the code of behaviour they represent has been tried and tested in the evolutionary struggle for survival."[5]

EVOLUTION AND THE NATURE OF GOOD

The philosophy profession in general tries to decide what ethical conduct is without reference to biology, and does not accept the existence of instinctive urges towards good behaviour from our inner selves. "It is a deep paradox of moral philosophy", writes Iris Murdoch, "that almost all philosophers have been led in one way or another to picture goodness as knowledge ..."[6] But the most primitive animals can be good, together with our more recent mammal and primate forbears; goodness comes before knowledge. "... we are moral agents before we are scientists ..."[7]

We need to lose the idea of absolute truth, with its resulting bigotry and mal-orientation to our needs, and to establish a basis on which to define absolute good—and so give a firm moral foundation from which to combat what is evil (leading to maladjustment) in our society, in place of the uncertain attitude which now leads to vacillating stances and ill-conceived tolerance of excesses.

Ethics in animals

Darwin himself worried deeply about the evolutionary meaning of morality, and many other people have shared his concern.[8] "Darwin argued that non-human animals have the same capacities that form the basis of morality in humans ...", writes James Rachels. "Morality is made possible, on Darwin's view, by our 'social instincts'—our natural disposition to act for the benefit of others. 'The moral sense', he wrote, 'is fundamentally identical with the social instincts.'"[9]   Much evidence has

ANCESTRAL DEVELOPMENT OF ETHICS

accumulated since Darwin on the moral behaviour of animals, including altruism in Rhesus monkeys.[10]

Midgley refers to the social nature of animals: "Far from being originally solitary, the earliest human beings were heirs to a long, complex tradition of group life, deep social affection and interdependence, a tradition which dates from many ages before their emergence as a separate species and their famous rise in intelligence... the special developments which raised their level of intelligence demanded of them ever more, not less, co-operation, affection, mutual help and interdependence.[11] ...we know from careful, unsentimental investigation that social traits like parental care, co-operative foraging and reciprocal kindness show that [birds and mammals] are not crude, exclusive egoists. They have evolved the strong and special motivations needed to form and maintain a simple society ..." Their activities include mutual grooming, mutual removal of parasites and mutual protection. "What makes them able to live together, and sometimes to co-operate in remarkable tasks of hunting, building, joint protection or the like, has to be their natural disposition to love and trust one another."[12] Carl Sagan and Ann Druyan remind us that "there is something like a code of ethics and morals operating among [chimps]—one that many human societies would find recognizable and, as far as it goes, congenial."[13]

Chimpanzees, says Mary Midgley, also set out to prevent social tension and vendettas: "... as [Frans] de Waal most interestingly reports, group-members who have quarrelled invariably do make peace [by approaching and comforting each other after one has attacked the other] before night, never letting the sun go down on their wrath."[14]

Ethics in hunter-gatherers

Brian Hayden draws attention to our ancestors' sense of community of property. "Perhaps the most pervasive characteristic [of generalised hunter-gatherers] is *sharing*. Anyone who brings food back to camp shares it with the immediate family and with anyone else who happens to be there or who asks for a share. No one is ever refused. Everyone in the community may obtain a portion if the quantity of food is enough to go around and if everyone wants some." Possessions are not closely identified with their current owners. "Giving was not altogether different from long-term lending, and theft was impossible... The custom of sharing is such a fundamental part of traditional hunter-gatherer life that it can create major problems for hunters who attempt to join the industrial world... In recent times, enterprising hunters who have worked hard to buy radios, binoculars and even cars have generally found that their 'brothers' [their community] soon come around to borrow those hard-won treasures. The man who has earned them cannot refuse: to do so would be to contravene the most fundamental ethic of the community and thus to renounce membership in the group...

"Why is sharing such an important value in hunter-gatherer societies? The limitation of the resource base and the fluctuation in supply provide the answer ... If all hunters were to hoard their kills selfishly, most people would be hungry most of the time. When everyone shares, though, individual variations in success in the hunt become averaged out, and everyone has enough food most of the time...

"Once people start claiming rights to things, self-centredness begins to take root, and soon people stop sharing food...

"When resources are limited and vulnerable to exploitation, *competition destroys the resource base*... Any hint of individualism or competition was ... severely suppressed... In fact, before the end of the Paleolithic we find *nothing* can be considered as a status or prestige item, nothing to indicate economically motivated competition, accumulation of wealth, or private ownership... Hunter-gatherers actively discouraged virtually any attitude that promoted the importance of the individual. This is probably the most difficult thing for people in industrial societies to comprehend. Even Richard Lee, who worked and lived among the !Kung Bushmen for years, was surprised by the reaction he got when he wanted to give a present to the bands with whom he worked, as an expression of his gratitude. For a summer solstice celebration, he went out and found the largest, fattest steer that was available in the area and treated the entire Bushman community to a feast the likes of which they had probably rarely seen. Lee was dumfounded when, instead of thanks, he got only comments in how sickly the steer looked, how thin it was, how tough the meat was, and what a silly waste the entire affair was. Then he realised that all these comments were standard responses to overly generous behaviour in Bushman society. For Bushmen view lavish gifts as attempts to exert control over others and to enhance the importance of the giver. Hunter-gatherers exert every effort to make sure that no individual assumes higher status than any other. The paramount value is the welfare of the group, and no individual can be permitted to threaten it."

Hayden concludes that (his italics) *it was natural selection that made co-operation part of human nature.*"[15]

Should we fall in with evolution or oppose it?

It is a popular idea that Nature is brutal, "red in tooth and claw", and that it is the destiny and duty of humans to overcome our animal nature and develop into a higher, more civilised form of life. Allied to this idea is a faith in advancing technology, and a belief that we can overcome all problems, including those caused by the advance of technology itself, by thinking of new ideas and achieving increasingly sophisticated technological methods. The first book in my series, *Evolution and the Spiral of Technology*, aims to expose the vanity of this idea and the threat posed by putting it into practice.[16] To oppose Nature *in perpetuo* is an increasingly complex and difficult task, and in time it will become impossible.

When we add to this the realization that co-operative, humane and sharing behaviour is inherent in *Homo*, and that our cultural development has been a deviation from our normal benign ethos and not a progressive improvement of morality, it becomes obvious that the right way, the light at the end of the tunnel, is to be found by recovering the co-operative nature of our forebears and trying, hard though it may be in our present state of sophistication, to become less dependent on competition. This is not a proposal that we should revert to some utopian state of "noble savagery"; it merely asks the reader to recognise that our race, like its ancestors, is naturally co-operative and sharing rather than competitive. As has been discussed in the book mentioned, and will be the subject of the last chapters of this book, the human cycle, like that of all animals, is a process of constant change; It is never possible to revert to a previous type, and in the particular case of humans we have to manage our future already loaded down with the freight of our acquired dependence on technology.

Limits to knowledge imposed by our evolution ensure that we can have no other concept of good than the welfare of humans and related species

The limits to what we can *know* have been discussed in my second book *Evolution and the Nature of Reality*.[17] Natural selection has honed us to be aware only of things that threaten or assist our survival; those things include our help to others. It follows that we can have no awareness of any good beyond the sense of good that we have inherited, that is, the interests of our fellows of various degrees of closeness.

EVOLUTION AND THE NATURE OF GOOD

The ethical sense is thus a purely subjective phenomenon; we act on it by instinct and not as a result of reasoning. Virginia Held writes: "Caring, empathy, feeling with others, being sensitive to each other's feelings, all may be better guides to what morality requires in actual contexts than many abstract rules of reason …"[18] When we take a bird's-eye view and relate our ethical instincts to their cause, which lies in our evolution, we can reach a rational conclusion about how they came about; however, the instincts themselves are subjective, they come from within us, and they are not the result of calculation.

Chapter 8

The nature of moral behaviour in the light of our evolutionary history

And now abideth faith, hope, charity, these three;
but the greatest of these is charity.
          St. Paul: *1 Corinthians 13.13*

The way we should behave, in a simple uncomplicated society, is fairly easily deduced if we accept the conclusions reached in the foregoing chapters. The purpose of this chapter is to summarise those conclusions and outline what they say about ethical behaviour. However, in the modern world life is much more complicated, and the complex culture that humans have developed interferes with the straightforward application of moral principles and the sort of behaviour that they dictate. These effects of our culture will be discussed in the last two chapters.

To recapitulate, therefore: First, our obligation is to people and other living beings. We have no obligation to non-living things, nor to deities or icons of any kind.

Secondly, our obligation is a contractual one and not a diffuse obligation to all the world. This is contrary to the view of utilitarianism, the "greatest good for the greatest number", which is in practice not calculable and impossible to achieve, and is based on non-biological thinking. Contracts are set up by all living things, and in the simplest form they are unwritten contracts with other members of the same species. Throughout the ages contracts have been of that type, inherited and inborn, and they include the contracts we have with our children and other relatives; some, however, are based on co-operation, in particular the contract between the parents that have to share responsibility for offspring. With the advent of culture in animals and humans we now have a second type of contract, the one to which the term is usually applied: namely an agreement (though usually not written down) between individuals, human or other, to engage in some activity together. The price agreed for a sale, or a bridge date, would be such a contract.

Thirdly, related to the second, our obligations are graded. Our greatest obligation is to those most closely related or most dependent on us, starting with our children and the spouse who helps us rear them. Beyond that we have duties to our parents, to more remote relatives, to our friends and neighbours, and to the whole human race, in descending order. Still further afield, we owe consideration to animals, in particular those with which we have close dealings such as dogs, cats and farm animals, but also to other animals such as sea and river fish: we have a common interest with them in that their survival helps to keep us in food. Finally, we have at the greatest reach an obligation to all other animals and all plants, because we depend for our survival and adjustment on the maintenance of a stable ecosphere.

We naturally fulfil these principles in our everyday lives; it is in general only when human-made cultural factors intervene that we have to stop and decide what is the right thing to do. Such factors include the urge to acquire and retain property, to win prestige and dominate economically, and to gratify inappropriate sexual feelings generated by our artificial mode of life.

The guiding principle in our interaction with other people is to be helpful without stopping to work out why we should—in a word, to be charitable, as recommended by St. Paul in his above-quoted letter to the Corinthians.

Meeting the needs of children

Chapter 4 has discussed the vital role played by women, which cannot be abandoned if we are to survive and prosper as a species.

Robert Wright highlights the need of families for sexual discipline before as well as during marriage. "If the Madonna-whore dichotomy is indeed firmly rooted in the male mind, then early sex with a woman may tend to stifle any budding feelings of love for her." Wright sees a need for both courtship and chastity.[1]

EVOLUTION AND THE NATURE OF GOOD

Courtship

When a wooer goes a-wooing,
Naught is truer than his joy.
Maiden hushing all his suing—
Boldly blushing—bravely coy!
Oh, the happy days of doing!
Oh, the sighing and the suing!
When a wooer goes a-wooing,
Oh, the sweets that never cloy!
    W.S. Gilbert, *The Yeomen of the Guard*

To Nature, what is required to raise children is a stable union
between two parents, and in the case of *Homo* Nature arranges
that they shall, if they are normal, unspoiled people, get to know
each other to some extent before they have sexual intercourse;
first they recognize common interests and later mutual
attraction. All pairing animals have a period of courtship, much
observed and studied in birds. The species that have evolved
long-term bonds are, by and large, the ones that rely on
elaborate courtship rituals. In well-adjusted people the urge for
copulation is actually inhibited until courtship has been
undertaken, as is suggested by the idea of "putting a girl on a
pedestal" and by the distinction between "nice girls" and
"beddable girls". At the end of it the pair know and accept each
other and the time is ripe to bear children. In this way Nature
protects children. Preparation for parenthood is the most
important part of education, though it does not feature largely in
the average school curriculum. Fortunately, the normal child
receives it without recourse to the classroom. It starts very early
in life with the formation of the love-bond between mother and

infant; as John Bowlby[2] and others have stressed, loved children make loving parents. It continues in early childhood in the form of warm relationships with any person in close contact with the child, and later with the experience of growing up in a united family in which parents stay together and live with each other in understanding and tolerance. When such a child reaches adolescence, she/he is ready to confront the greatest challenge of life: to start the process of selecting a mate with whom she/he can live permanently in order to rear a family in proper security. The normal teenager is not motivated merely to try out the new-found sexual prowess; inter-sex relationships evolve slowly in a well-adjusted child. Nature has provided *Homo* with the means to seek and find a suitable partner through a prolonged period of discovery and courtship. Often the first dawning of sexual maturity is accompanied by a surge of altruism—an urge to do something selfless, to help the human race as a whole or some needy group within it.

At the same time, the current mores are important, and if even a well-adjusted adolescent sees that indiscriminate sex is the "in" thing, he/she is more likely to practise it even if it against his/her own overall inclination.

Chastity

No human trait is more rejected or ridiculed in contemporary writing and media productions than chastity. No smart-hero kit is complete without at least one casual love affair, no heroine properly emancipated unless she has a tumble or two in the course of the saga. The offender against chastity, whether married or not, is not cast as the villain, unlike the murderer or robber whose misdeeds will usually catch up with him in due course. Nor are sexual lapses portrayed in great heart-rending epics in which the agonized human spirit is torn between love and duty. They usually come, like brandy after dinner, as a pleasant way to end an eventful and rather tiring day.

Chastity does not deserve such treatment, for it is the glue of our society, the matrix in which the process of socialization has been built up. It is imposed in many—probably most—primitive human societies and in some it is scrupulously observed, with very serious penalties for violation.

Wright recognizes the huge importance for children of lasting marriages, and cites Darwin, who "once worried that contraceptive technology would 'spread to unmarried women and would destroy chastity on which the family bond depends; & the weakening of this bond would be the greatest of all possible evils to mankind.' … it is harder now than it would have been thirty years ago to dismiss Darwin's fear as the ranting of an ageing Victorian."[3]

Bowlby, in his book *Child Care and the Growth of Love* written after the second world war[4] gives a well-researched and very convincing argument that children have a need for continuous loving care from their mother in particular, and also from their father, if they are to grow up happy and well-adjusted. It is easy to wonder if a life of sexual freedom engaged in before marriage causes people to go into marriage insufficiently oriented, prepared and committed to want, give birth to and rear children and to stay together, for that purpose,

MORAL BEHAVIOUR IN LIGHT OF EVOLUTION

for the rest of their lives. Those of our animal relations that form families and rear their young do not engage in sex without reproductive consequences, nor before they are ready to raise their young; their whole pursuit of courtship and mating is directed towards the production and rearing of offspring.

Wright says that since 1977, "women, who have much leverage over sexual morality, have, in apparently growing numbers, asked basic questions about the wisdom of highly casual sex."[5]

In these days many couples decide to bear and bring up children without having a formal marriage ceremony. What matters biologically is not that they are married in the eyes of the law, but that when they form a sexual relationship they are fully committed to each other and to the children they will have. The lack of a formal marriage in no way exonerates them from the responsibilities associated with marriage. I am reminded of that sad little song of fidelity which in my youth was regarded as a little comic and bawdy:

> Now I was bachelor, I lived all alone, and I worked at
> the weaver's trade,
> And the only, only thing that I ever did wrong was to woo
> a fair young maid.
> I wooed her in the winter time, and in the summer too,
> And the only, only thing that I ever did wrong was to
> save her from the foggy, foggy dew.

> Now I am a bachelor, I live with my son, and we work at
> the weaver's trade,
> And every, every time that I look into his eyes he
> reminds me of that fair young maid.
> He reminds me of the winter time, and of the summer too,
> When I took her into bed, and I covered up her head, just
> to save her from the foggy, foggy dew.

EVOLUTION AND THE NATURE OF GOOD

Spouse

The chief responsibility for ethical behaviour between marital partners falls on the man. Women have evolved to be dependent on a constant relationship because of their responsibility for their children, and this dependence is not only material but emotional also. Men, because of their evolved role primarily as fertilizers, have a greater tendency to stray in body and mind and look for new partners; from the evolutionary point of view this gives them more chance to continue their gene line.

The evil of divorce, or separation of partners, rests in the harm it may do to people. Clearly the people most affected are the children of the union; if there are no children the separation cannot harm them. As well as the children, however, the other party to the union must be considered. To meet the needs of the children a marriage needs to last 20 years or more. Many years of living together and sharing responsibilities produce a bond between people. While one partner may in time tire of the relationship and wish to end it, the other may well have become very dependent on it. More often the latter is the woman. The discontented party retains an obligation towards the dependent one. Inherited differences between women and men mean that women have need of help from men, and women are dependent on sexual restraint. Divorce is very often a raw deal for women.[6]

MORAL BEHAVIOUR IN LIGHT OF EVOLUTION

Other relatives

Since the hominids re-adopted the pair-bond, our ancestors have made much use of close kin and the local community in helping to look after their children, more recently coming to depend on grandparents—who have, since Cro-Magnon days, lived long enough to be of service. This has continued right up to recent times. Elderly individuals are also important as repositories of experience.[7] Before people were drawn to the mines and cities by industry, families as they grew stayed in the same place and worked the same piece of land. To pre-industrial societies, as Alvin Toffler says, "Working together assured, if nothing else, tight, complex, 'hot' personal relationships—a committedness many people envy today."[8]

Those with whom we have innate or agreed contracts

We also have a heavy obligation to those on whom we depend for cooperation[9]—the outstanding example being the spouse whose children we share, mentioned above.

Other humans

Other people are the members of our own species. It is a direct consequence of natural selection that members of a species do not destroy each other. They may disable each other temporarily in competition for mates, thus ensuring that the strongest genes are passed on, but they do not set out to kill their fellows.

EVOLUTION AND THE NATURE OF GOOD

Modern *Homo* is the only animal that does this. Yet it is in our nature to help and co-operate with all other peoples, and it is in our interests to do so.

Other animals

Many animals are our partners in life, both farm stock and domestic animals such as horses, dogs and cats. To drown a kitten is very unpleasant to the average human. To most people it is abhorrent to attack an animal, especially a mammal with blood and red flesh. We are much less bothered about swatting insects, though if they are not being a great nuisance we will probably choose to leave them be. Reptiles fall between mammals and insects. These attitudes reflect the different degrees of obligation that we have to the various classes of animal.

The ecosphere as a whole

Finally, we have an obligation to the whole living world, including that huge majority of it which is plants. The interest of humans lies in maintaining the world in a constant state, as near as possible to its condition at the time that our species was born. It is clear that we have miserably failed to do that. Our accelerating culture has been accompanied by accelerating change in the surface of the Earth and in the air. We pay lip-service to the "Environment", and adopt pious schemes to recycle, but these are far too little, far too late. For instance,

MORAL BEHAVIOUR IN LIGHT OF EVOLUTION

every day that we return some carefully gathered paper to the system, most households in Britain buy a newspaper the size of a book whose contents contribute nothing towards preserving the ecosphere. We are failing in our duty towards the world as a whole, and the best thing we can do to put that right is to simplify our lives and demand less resources.

PART IV
TECHNOLOGICAL ADVANCE AND ETHICS

Chapter 9
The impact of technological advance on ethical principles

Selfishness is at the bottom of civilization.
Senator Henry L. Dawes, Massachusetts, 1908[1]

Up to this point we have been considering the rules for ethical behaviour as they have come down to us from our ancestors. With the rapid advance of human culture, however, these rules cannot now be simply applied. The use of simple tools by palaeolithic *Homo* was followed by the adoption of farming, a resulting great increase of population and population density, competition for material goods, the stratification of society into classes, and the industrial, scientific and electronic revolutions. This chapter considers how the new milieu interferes with the application of the moral code dictated by our genetic and traditional inheritance.

IMPACT OF TECHNOLOGY ON ETHICAL PRINCIPLES

The rise of human culture

The problem of adapting to changes we have produced

The modern human genetic make-up is very much that of hunter-gatherer peoples. *Homo* was a hunter-gatherer for 99% of its existence; only over the past 12,000 years has it acquired, by degrees, a settled mode of life. This period is too short for significant genetic changes to take place; yet during it, through our own agency, our environment has changed out of all recognition. The changes occurred relatively slowly at first, but now so fast that the environment is different from one generation to the next. The result is that we live in a world quite different from the one for which our genes have prepared us. We are faced with the very challenging task of fitting ourselves to the greatly altered environment we have created.

As has been discussed in Chapter 5, the increase in the world's population and the large units in which it is now, as a result, arranged, mean that the social relationships which have been with *Homo* over its millions of years of evolution have been sharply changed in the last ten thousand years or so. Our community sizes are far greater than those we are genetically designed for, which are hunter-gatherer groups of about 50-100 people. These early tribal groups were small enough for everyone to know everyone else.

EVOLUTION AND THE NATURE OF GOOD

The technology spiral

Brian Hayden defines five key developments in human history:
1. Technology and a hunter-gatherer lifestyle
2. Resource based competition and the production (rather than the acquisition) of food
3. Class societies
4. The Industrial Revolution
5. The nuclear/cybernetics revolution.[2]

"We are caught [in the spiral of cultural and technological advance]... the system has taken on a life of its own and structured human interests in such a fashion that basic elements cannot be eliminated without massive destruction and misery that no one will willingly tolerate.[3]... Through one of those ironies of evolution, some of the most radical changes are instigated by attempts to keep things the same while surrounding conditions change... Mesolithic hunter-gatherers [10-11,000 years ago] were almost certainly attempting to preserve their way of life, the only one they knew. In developing new technologies to that end, however, they unwittingly tapped into a new dimension of resources that dramatically transformed their traditional way of life and unleashed an entirely new, extremely powerful evolutionary force [Hayden is referring here to cultural, not genetic evolution] almost unknown in human existence up to that point—a force that was to dominate human evolution from that time through the nuclear age. They had opened Pandora's box and released forces that today threaten to destroy the world. It is almost as if these Mesolithic hunter-gatherers were being drawn gradually into another dimension through a black hole, or had evoked some primal force. The name of the force they released is *economic competition*."[4]

Competition

Serious competition began in the Mesolithic. Technology was adapted to display the importance of an individual, and prestige technology was added to practical technology.

After farming and settlement began, people established semi-permanent villages and began to compete socioeconomically with their surplus food and labour, both within and between villages. These were the *complex* hunter-gatherers.[5] It was the onset of plenty that made people selfish.

"In the whole of human development, only two major forces have been responsible for directional changes in human adaptations: *resource stress* and *competition*." Hayden believes that whereas resource stress may in the first instance give rise to competition, the habit of competition persists even when resources are again plentiful. "Over the past several decades industrial society has undergone change at an unprecedented rate with virtually no resource stress whatsoever, at least not to the extent that any significant number of communities are dying from starvation or malnutrition. The industrial world has developed plastics, computers, space travel, nuclear energy, and thousands of offshoot bits of technology while maintaining the highest standard of living ever known in human history. It is simply meaningless to talk of resource stress or starvation for the general populations of industrial societies. If resource stress is not driving the engine of cultural change in contemporary society, what is?

"There can be little doubt that the force behind this rapid rate of change is competition. I believe that what we find, both in this case and in the case of the Mesolithic hunter-gatherers, is that competition becomes an important [cultural] evolutionary force when sought-after resources suddenly become abundant. Competition is intense because control of ... the resources ... may determine who will come out ahead in the game of evolution. Though most people are not usually conscious of the evolutionary implications of their actions, they are generally aware of the immediate benefits of increasing the resources under their control and of the potential risk of being displaced, absorbed or killed should rivals gain control of new resources. Elizabeth Cashdan ..., who has studied modern Bushmen, has documented the remarkable rapidity with which generalized, egalitarian hunter-gatherers can be transformed into competitive, wealth-seeking individuals by the establishment of more stable and abundant resources.

"These ... principles ... are exceedingly important for understanding how and why human cultures have changed, and what forces continue to affect our own culture today." [6]

Competitive feasting was the key to acquiring control over surplus food, wealth and power. "... such feasts would have provided a strong motive to produce ever greater quantities of food of ever more impressive size and quality."[7]

IMPACT OF TECHNOLOGY ON ETHICAL PRINCIPLES

Big Men

The main social characteristic of the Neolithic, when agriculture began, was the emergence of Big Men. With storage, they could dominate community life. "... when one understands that ... gifts had to be returned with interest, and that indebtedness was a technique to gain influence and control over people, competitive feasting behaviour makes perfect sense."[8] Big Men had to start by influencing people since they began from a sharing culture, and they then used this influence to acquire power. Because each Big Man tries to top the last feast that was held, "competitive feasting is intensely *inflationary*."[9] (This type of self-advertisement is less incredible when you look at modern advertising.)

Chiefs

Hayden describes the development of socially and economically stratified chiefdoms from the egalitarian Big Man feasting societies, a key stage in human history. "Socioeconomically stratified societies no longer rely on the feast as the principal means of gaining acquiescence in the elites' designs, although feasts continue to structure power relationships in a slightly modified way. One of the major differences between egalitarian Big Man feasting societies and socioeconomically stratified chiefdoms is that the chief has much more economic leverage than the traditional Big Man; the equilibrium point in the system of checks and balances has clearly shifted in the direction of men who aspire to greatness and to promoting their own self-interest. They are able to mobilise far more community resources to construct monumental buildings, undertake irrigation and other public works, hold slaves, sacrifice human lives, and generally extend their wealth, privileges, and power. As a result of this shift in power, ambitious men acquire all but exclusive control over economic resources for themselves and their supporters."[10] Ancestor worship was used by the chiefs to entrench their status and power.

"The Big Man had to work hard himself to get everyone else to play his social dominance game, but the chief has so much power that he no longer has to do much menial work."[11]

"Finally, remember that the emergence of chiefdoms depended on two things: first, an abundant resource base capable of supporting specialists, elaborate administrations, and intense economic competition; and second, restricted access to some vital resources."[12]

Stratification of society and the formation of élites

The increase in size of population groups gave rise to the need for organized government; there had to be rulers and ruled, commanders and obeyers, and society became layered into different orders, higher and lower, who became inevitably the privileged and the plebs, the haves and the have-nots.

The chiefs gathered ruling élites round them. "The families that have the greatest control over resources constitute an élite or noble class. Elites can act as administrators for large corporate groups of commoners, as in the case of chiefs of clans; or they may have no lasting ties or obligations to others, as in the case of owners of companies in industrial societies. The reasons that stratified societies emerged should be of great interest to us because our own society is stratified."[13]

"As in contemporary societies, wars are started by those who stand to profit most from the outcome: the élites."[14]

Further competition and the exploitation of resources

With the exploitation of metals, people became yet more aggressive and competitive, trying to amass as much wealth for themselves as they could. Raiders destroyed villagers rather than come to terms with them; they could find metals without their co-operation.[15]

The Indo-European scramble for metal and other resources created a social climate in which it was self-destructive not to compete. "Thus many people see no alternative to going along with the forces of rugged individualism and competition if they are to survive in any reasonable fashion under conditions of expanding resource opportunities.[16]...Like the expansion of the pastoral Indo-European nomads, the Bantu expansion that began in western Africa and ultimately encompassed nearly all of sub-Saharan Africa was associated with herding and the introduction of iron.[17]... Colonial and contemporary societies have learned how to extract and transform resources into valued industrial items at an exponentially increasing rate until they have engulfed the world. In many respects, we have continued the Indo-European adaptation, displacing weaker communities in order to obtain their resources."[18]

The acquisition of selfishness

With the formation of élites, they "explored every excess that communities would tolerate—slavery, sacrifice, enforced exploitation of the least powerful segments of the community." The benefit of the increased productivity accrued to the elites.[19] Like the chiefs before them, the élites of states had voracious appetites for human resources. They exploited labour and entrepreneurs so that the greatly increased production benefited them but made things worse for those under them. They "also emphasized monocropping, the production of huge amounts of single crops of starchy staples that would feed the largest number of people at the lowest cost, regardless of nutritional value."[20]

Their attitude continues to the present day. "If the vast majority of people in industrial nations now can live better than kings of the past and are still not satisfied, one wonders if human beings can ever be satisfied as long as they think there may be something more to be had. When do we say that we have had enough? Will we ever be content with what we have, or will our voracious appetites impel us to consume the resources of this world, and perhaps others, until almost nothing is left?"[21] For the ancient people of Sumer, "Sad to say, this very passion for competition and success carried within it the seeds of destruction and decay."[22]

The selfish behaviour of Big Men and chiefs is no worse than that of modern corporations, which exist solely for the benefit of shareholders and aim at profits regardless of the effect on people of any kind, as long as they are not prevented by the law.

The essential problem that modern humans have to confront is that, as Hayden explains, a culture of mutual aid has given place to a culture of selfishness. Earlier, progressively increasing socialization and mutual help characterized the evolution of mammals, apes, hominids and palaeolithic *Homo*. Our own culture has greatly increased the pace of change, introducing private enterprise and capitalism, and a way of relating to each other based on bargaining and an improvement of our own material circumstances. Deviations from ethical behaviour occur as a result of culture; this is already seen in apes, who may act in a way to deceive others for their own advantage. In humans the selfish approach has reached an extreme degree, and the accepted mode of our social intercourse in westernized nations is by arrangements that will result in mutual profit. It is not possible for people who interact in such huge numbers to do so in the traditional co-operative way, and this becomes a substitute. Personal advantage is regarded as the primary aim. The embodied system of selfishness has been extended so that many people use it not only to achieve fair arrangements between themselves but to cheat.

The contrast between natural feelings and the mind-set induced by technological advance and dogma

Jonathan Bennett describes the characters of three people, one fictional and two real, each of whom presents a different aspect of the conflict between the customary behaviour in one's sophisticated environment and the exercise of natural human feelings.

Huckleberry Finn had a friend, Jim, who was a slave, and helped him to escape. He was deeply worried because he felt he was stealing the slave from his owner, a nice old lady, and also because Jim declared his intention of stealing his brother and sister from their owner and freeing them. Huck felt he was abetting robbery.

Heinrich Himmler oversaw the slaughter of many millions of Jews, Russians and Czechs. It was accepted behaviour in the Nazi party. Yet Himmler was aware that a person's natural feelings may mitigate against such a programme; he expressed these feelings himself, and his concern that his fellows and underlings in the task might, because of having to do the work, lose all feeling and destroy like automatons. Many did, in fact, but Himmler praised "the stronger and more glorious course of retaining one's sympathies while acting in violation of them." Himmler suffered a variety of nervous and physical disabilities.

The clash between the moral sense and religious dogma has been mentioned on page 30. Jonathan Edwards, the evangelist, did some good work, but his moral philosophy was worse than Himmler's. "According to Edwards, God condemns some men to an eternity of unimaginably awful pain, though he arbitrarily spares others, although none deserve to be spared. It seems that he did not even have any sympathies which conflicted with this philosophy. The angels delight in the eternal torment of the damned."[23]

Interaction of selfishness with the further advance of technology

Quite early in the industrial revolution, Robert Owen was deeply concerned about the long labouring shifts in factories and the loss of health and dignity suffered by workers. Factory employment, he said, had become merely a cash relationship regardless of moral responsibility, and this moral abdication was for him what mattered most. "All", Owen wrote, "are sedulously trained to buy cheap and sell dear; and to succeed in this art, the parties must be taught to acquire strong powers of deception [well seen in modern advertising]; and thus a spirit is generated through every class of traders, destructive of that open, honest, sincerity, without which man cannot make others happy, nor enjoy happiness himself."[24]

EVOLUTION AND THE NATURE OF GOOD

Moral deterioration through the loss of close acquaintance

The growth of communities has led to the loss of mutual acquaintance as a basis for co-operation, and given rise to the ideas of ownership, property, rights, money and capital.[25] Cheating the system is morally much easier since one does it impersonally and not to a particular individual. Killing with a gun is cleaner and easier than using bare hands or even a knife.[26] Genocide as a policy of governments has been possible because the population as a whole do not know the group that is killed, and also—because of the high level of organization—it is possible to whip up xenophobia against them.[27] Robert Wright notes that integrity and honesty make particular sense in a small and steady social setting, where there are pressures from others to conform to them. Character (which, according to Samuel Smiles, means truthfulness, integrity and goodness), has in the twentieth century been replaced by personality (charm, pizzazz and other social garnish).[28]

The drive for industrial productivity is damaging to personal relations

The organization of the technological society prevents the formation of mutually familiar, communicating and supportive communities. In his book *Tools for Conviviality*[29] Ivan Illich denounces our system of industrial productivity as inimical to conviviality (literally "living together"), which he defines as autonomous and creative intercourse among persons and the

IMPACT OF TECHNOLOGY ON ETHICAL PRINCIPLES

intercourse of persons with their environment. In Illich's view, these fundamental and natural human activities are pre-empted and excluded by a raft of mass production enterprises, including education, public transport, communication, health services, welfare, and national defence, each of which produces a service commodity, each organised as a public utility and each defining its output as a basic necessity; and each eventually imposes its use upon its consumers.

Democracy and politics

Democracy is not an absolute good, but a system of government that seems to be the best when society has reached a state like ours: containing large numbers of people in a unit, and able to understand and respect the workings of a democratic state.

Democracy is introduced as a result of a revolution, violent or peaceful, which overthrows some despotic regime that has become too oppressive. At its start, therefore, it meets the *needs* of the people. Those earlier societies, human or non-human, in which democracy was introduced before the acceleration of modern human culture, had no excess of resources, and so the introduction of the system meant that needed resources were distributed more equally through the community. The effect of democracy in our affluent society, however, has been that people's *wants* rather than their needs are satisfied, and this often results in effects that are bad for them.

Politicians always pander to the wants of people and do not look to their needs. Modern government is incapable of working for the long-term good of people for this reason. When trying to deal with problems caused by the technology spiral, including damage to the environment, global warming, bad eating habits and lack of exercise, governments are ineffective because of their motivation to stay in power and avoid introducing unpopular measures. What such administrations as those of the US and Britain never do is to look to the real interests of people.

Economics

Hayden points to the acquisitive attitude caused by economics. "Make no mistake about it, in the short run, industrial products make work easier, life more healthy and enjoyable, and survival surer. People everywhere crave these benefits, and in this respect, all peoples are intensely materialistic, contrary to the claims of some idealists in our own society."[30]

Fritjof Capra argues that economics has become divorced from real human needs. "The motive of individual gain from economic activities was generally absent [before Adam Smith and the Enlightenment]; the very idea of profit, let alone interest, was either inconceivable or banned."[31] Adam Smith's economic philosophy is based on reductionism, and makes no provision for human drives, quirks and emotions. Capra believes that the idea of continual growth is utterly unrealistic. The economics of both Marx and Keynes, he says, is rooted in reductionism and now out of date.[32]

Capra points out the danger of uncontrolled technological growth. "...very often the side effects of the 'solution' are more harmful than the original problem[33] ... If the consequences of corporate power are harmful in the industrialized countries, they are altogether disastrous in the Third World[34] ... Free markets, balanced by supply and demand, have long disappeared; they exist only in our economics textbooks."[35]

How does the growth of GDP (the gross domestic product of a nation) interact with biology? How does the growth come about? What does capital represent in terms of our real possessions? The world is finite in size, so when someone owns something does it mean someone else owns less?   Is wealth correlated with happiness and adjustment?

The GDP is bound up with the technology spiral. Western people, especially since the Industrial Revolution, have started to *make* things out of raw materials instead of simply *consuming* them, and nowadays there are many stages in the preparation of manufactured goods. Each stage involves a transaction, and each sale adds to the GDP. An increase in the GDP, therefore, is simply a reflection of the acceleration of human life, the technology spiral, and the transition from meeting *needs* to meeting *wants*.

Diane Coyle's book *The Soulful Science*[36] claims to approach economics broadly, and as a subject concerned with ethics. She invokes chaos theory, complexity and emergence, and the role of society, but does not relinquish the traditional view of economists that the increase of GDP is a good thing and the aim of economics is to achieve it. She makes several references to Darwin and to evolutionary theory, but considers natural selection to be purely a process of competition, without consideration of the co-operation within species that is so important a part of it. Although co-operation and altruism are mentioned she does not see them as the product of our ancestors' nature. She quotes authors who believe that these competitive principles of natural selection may be applicable to other human activities, notably economics. The errors here are twofold: first, natural selection is purely a genetic mechanism and does not work on cultural activities; and second, she does not see the enormous part that co-operation, as opposed to competition, has played in the evolution of mammals and particularly of humankind.

Economists generally do not recognize that continual growth is unsustainable; but it must either lead to some sort of crisis in the long run, or suffer reversals from time to time to restore a measure of equilibrium. Morally, for the real needs of *Homo*, the aim of economics at any time should be *not* the growth of GDP but the constant regulation and adjustment of inequalities in the access of different social groups (in general, classes at different levels of prosperity) to sufficient material goods to maintain a manageable and satisfying life within the prevailing state of society.

IMPACT OF TECHNOLOGY ON ETHICAL PRINCIPLES

The abuse of animals in modern farming

Peter Singer points out that by far the worst abuses of animals are committed on farm stock, and gives a vivid description of the mistreatment they suffer as a result of the adoption of mass production methods. "Animals are treated like machines that convert low-priced fodder into high-priced flesh, and any innovation will be used if it results in a cheaper 'conversion ratio'." He refers to the keeping of battery hens and pigs, the artificial, mechanised lives imposed on cattle to maximise milk and beef production, and the transportation of animals. There is a detailed description of the production of veal from anaemic calves kept away from their mothers in tiny crates all their lives.[37] All this cruelty, to which we scarcely give a thought at our meal-tables, is the result of technological advance, mechanisation and mass production.

Alteration of the environment

Violations of ethical behaviour include the way we handle the biosphere, and the damage we do to people other than ourselves and animals by altering the environment—all results of the drive for profit. In the Third World, commerce-driven farming and the profit-driven use of land are cases in point. The effects on the social environment, as well as the physical, are very important.

The unpalatable fact is that all humans are already committed to doing much harm by the extent to which we have become

142

EVOLUTION AND THE NATURE OF GOOD

The disruption of family life

Of all the human needs which today's mass society fails to
meet, two stand out from the rest: love and a sense of belonging.
Patrick Rivers, *The Survivalists*[38]

Jonathan Sacks, the Chief Rabbi of the United Hebrew
Congregations of the British Commonwealth, expressed deep
concern about the future of the family in his book *Faith in the
Future*.[39] "Today three out of every ten children are born
outside of marriage. One in five is brought up in a one-parent
family. Almost four in ten marriages end in divorce. There are
inner-city areas in Britain and the US where the stable nuclear
family is almost unknown... There have been protests ...
against the erosion of the natural environment, and they have
been loud and long. But there has been no equivalent protest at
the erosion of our human environment, the world of
relationships into which we bring our children... Assisted by
birth control, abortion, new work patterns and the liberalisation
of all laws and constraints touching on relationships, we have
divorced sex from love, love from commitment, marriage from
having children, and having children from responsibility for
their care... Seeing something of ourselves live on in our
children is the nearest we come in this life to immortality...
Our children are now born into a world of unprecedentedly
rapid change, economic, political and technological. They do
not have what most people at most times have had: a set of

stable expectations about what they will do and experience and become."[40]

Reduction to the nuclear family

In Alvin Toffler's "Second Wave"—the Industrial Revolution—family structure began to change. "Torn apart by migration to cities, battered by economic storms," Toffler writes, "families stripped themselves of unwanted relatives, grew smaller, more mobile, and more suited to the needs of the new techno-sphere... The nuclear family became an identifiable feature of all Second Wave societies ...".[41] Westerners are inclined to think of the nuclear family as the norm; but for Robert Ardrey, "The family was never the windowless chamber as the Freudians saw it except in isolated, insecure arrangements of *Homo sapiens*... The adult who asks [about the revolt of the young] 'Why now?' must recall that only since the Second World War have technological advances, together with the vast organization of technological empires, reduced the family as a unit to microscopic scale."[42] Families fail, John Bowlby writes, largely because of the fragmentation of industrial society into nuclear family units. "In many of the economically less-developed communities, people live in large family groups made up of three or four generations. Near and known relatives—grandmothers, aunts, older sisters—are thus always at hand to take the maternal role in an emergency.

"Economic support, moreover, is forthcoming if the breadwinner is incapacitated. The greater family group living together in one locality provides a social insurance system of great value. Even in Western communities, there are many rural pockets in which close-knit and much intermarried village groups provide similar social services for their members." In industrial areas, "Despite social break-up, it still remains the tradition (though less strongly than formerly), that if [the mother-father group] fails for any reason, near relatives take responsibility for the child."[43]

Break-up of the family

Ardrey believes that "It is technology, man's Frankenstein, that is destroying it [(the family)]."[44]   Mary and John Gribbin define two new cultural pressures that have worked against the family unit as our technology-based society has developed. (1) one man and one woman—or one woman on her own—have become well able, in material terms, to raise several children, thanks to inventions such as agriculture and machine technology. (2) The community as a whole is now able to take on all or part of the burden of child-rearing, through crèches, nursery schools and schools, releasing women almost entirely from what has been their primary biological function since the mammalian line began.[45]   Bowlby says that the full-time employment of mothers is among the causes of the natural home group failing to care for the child.[46] "... the mother of young children is not free, or at least should not be free, to earn ...".[47]   Toffler says that in the United States in 1980 "...

IMPACT OF TECHNOLOGY ON ETHICAL PRINCIPLES

we find the vast majority—as many as two-thirds to three-quarters of the population—living outside the nuclear situation."[48] E.O. Wilson gives statistics of family break-up in the US: "The nuclear family, based on long-term sexual bonding, geographical mobility, and female domesticity, is declining at this moment in the United States. Between 1967 and 1977 the divorce rate doubled, and the number of households headed by women increased by a third. In 1977 one of every three school children lived in a home headed by only one parent or relative, and more than half of all mothers with school-age children worked outside the home. Day-care centres have come to replace the parents in many working families: their older offspring constitute a large population of 'latchkey' children who are wholly unsupervised in the period between the end of school and the parents' return from work." But, Wilson says, the traditional nuclear family is deeply rooted in our nature and repeatedly asserts itself.[49] The estimated proportion of children reported as maltreated in the US rose from 10.1 per thousand in 1976 to 47.0 per thousand 1n 1996. US youth suicides (at ages 15-24) rose from 8.8 per 100,000 in 1970 to 14.0 in 1994, but fell to 12.0 by 1996. There was a similar trend in violent crime, which increased from 363 per 100,000 in 1970 to 745 in 1992, but had decreased to 634 by 1996. Perhaps there is a ray of hope in these last two statistics, which may lend support to Wilson's claim that we instinctively return to family values.[50]

EVOLUTION AND THE NATURE OF GOOD

The decline of loving care for children

John Bowlby's studies have made it clear how important a mother is to her young children, not only in her presence but also in her attitude, which traditionally is that her children are her prime concern.

Parents are distracted from their primary family obligation. The cycle of development engenders restlessness. Men are affected and want to relieve the boredom of the day by going to the local, seeing friends or playing golf; or if in management or a profession they may be unable to put their work down, and bring it home. Men come to under-value their families and are tempted to look further afield for excitement, which may be of a sexual nature.

But it is when women are afflicted by this restlessness that the family faces the greatest risk of disruption, since they are the pivotal unit in the family structure. In 1947, 28% of Britain's working population were women; this proportion rose progressively to 43% in 1993. Some women have sufficient emotional security and maternal drive to weather the stresses added by a working life and yet retain the full commitment to their children that the children need and recognize; but there are many who are overwhelmed by the demanding combination.

Failure of communication between parents and children

Apart from the distraction of modern parents by their interests outside the home, referred to above, television prevents social intercourse and inhibits contact between parents and children. With four people in a room it is almost impossible to switch it off at any time without causing trouble.   On the use of computers by growing children, Melvin Konner remarks that if something other than the parents responds to the actions of a child systematically, this could destroy a part of its capacity for human social life.[51] The strong attachments formed nowadays between some young people and computers may come into this category.

The loss of taboos

A leading feature of our modern culture is that taboos are taboo, and the greatest pariahs are the sexual ones. Strong sexual taboos exist in other species, especially hunters, which depend, like our species, on mutual cooperation within the species.

Incest taboos we observe, and they are universal among animals; as Sagan and Druyan say, "... a high-priority, well-functioning incest taboo is operating among the chimps ...",[52] our nearest relatives. We maintain it in law because we can see that abnormalities arise in the offspring of incestuous couplings. It is usually not difficult. The "kibbutz phenomenon" showed that children who knew each other before the age of six are inhibited against developing sexual attraction to each other; they did not mate, nor even have casual sex.[53] The Gribbins remark that "This is especially interesting because in 'prudish' Victorian societies boys and girls are kept apart and not allowed to play together, even within the same biological family. And this can have exactly the opposite of the intended effect ...!"[54]

We have been much less careful about our other sexual taboos, against casual encounters, frequent changes of partner, and copulation with no thought of having children or forming a permanent relationship, because the ill-effects of violating them are much less obvious and measurable. Lechers and journalists alike are quick to take advantage of the scientific attitude that a theory should not be believed or acted on until it is proven. Modern society is dominated by rationality—there has to be an explainable reason for every restraint. The older generation that would maintain the taboos cannot defend their stance. Yet these taboos have become a part of the structure of society that keeps it in equilibrium. Their violation means that the whole fabric of our society is threatened with disruption of family life and the emotional neglect of children.

Anti-social behaviour in children

There is much discussion in the newspapers and on the radio of the problems the education system in the UK is confronting due to bad discipline and the disruption caused by some children. Various causes and remedies are discussed, for instance, does the onus for good behaviour of children fall upon the parents? Is corporal punishment right? It is suggested that the law should forbid parents to smack their children. Teachers are blamed for the failure of discipline, and there is talk of culling bad teachers.

The underlying problem is not confronted because it is politically incorrect; families that fail to form proper internal relationships do so because parents do not want or do not love their children, and the reason for this is largely their preoccupation with worldly matters outside the family. "Many technological societies", writes Jonathan Kingdon, "have gone so far that parents can diminish, shed or even renounce their responsibilities as parents altogether. This cuckoo syndrome is a luxury that can only be temporary."[55]

The failure of discipline

Many modern parents have come to confuse the imposition of discipline with lack of love, and do not ask children to conform to their standards. Children, who normally expect guidance and firmness from their parents, quickly become aware of this indecision and the lack of a restraining hand, and may respond by taking even more licence. Though evidently less important than an actual failure of parental affection, this lack of firmness, assisted by the extent of change that now takes place in twenty-five years in the world we live in, contributes to the "generation gap". A 1995 report *Psychosocial disorders in young people*, edited by Michael Rutter and David Smith and reviewed by Nick Cohen in the London *Independent on Sunday* newspaper of 4th June 1995, draws attention to the effect of freedom allowed inappropriately by parents and by society, and its link with crime in young people. Rutter and Smith found that every problem studied—crime, suicide, depression, eating disorders, and alcohol and drug abuse—showed a substantial rise among young people since the second world war. This, they say, is not primarily due to poverty and unemployment. Freedom permitted inappropriately becomes a synonym for neglect. Cohen concludes that "The real 20th-century revolution in most Western countries is the collapse in traditional family structures and the ending of sexual and social taboos." On the same day there was an article in *The Observer* about the Rutter report by Melanie Phillips, who comments that both Left and Right have encouraged libertarian individualism, the latter largely through promoting the free play of self-interest in the market. The adult world has retreated from the young, she says. The philosophy of freedom for youth has been the excuse for parents to relinquish their responsibility and pursue their own interests. Teachers have reacted the same way. Love has been turned into an expression of self-interest. Real parenting means care and control.

The complexity of ethics caused by technological advance

The development of human culture has enormously complicated the application of moral principles. The reason is that we have become progressively dependent on every change (or "advance") that we have made in our way of life.

We of the western democracies owe a huge moral debt to certain groups at whose expense we have acquired our life-style: non-human members of the biosphere; people whose exploitation makes our "high" standard of living possible, and at the same time deprives them of adequate basic necessities; people whose adoption of the mass organization spawned by western culture has placed them at the mercy of thugs, whether tyrannical politicians or hooligans who are out of the control of the police; and those who have been moved out of their accustomed environments or deprived of their traditional support by the functioning of western society, such as, in Africa, miners and other employees and their families.

Simple ethics as indicated by the recognition of our place in the biosphere is complicated in the technological world by our acquired dependency on the sophisticated environment. We usually cannot at any point drop a practice that is unnatural and harmful or cruel to other members of the biosphere, because it would damage us and our dependants. Ethical behaviour has to be calculated, reaching a compromise between, on the one hand, adaptive moral behaviour on the assumption that we had not complicated and sophisticated our lives, and on the other, making provision for the distortions that modern life has produced. For instance, you cannot simply say that people who have become dependent on cars to get to work should individually abandon them and stay at home. What is it right for such a person to do?

For this reason ethical decisions are often complicated and difficult, requiring a balance to be struck between the requirements of nature and the culturally-acquired needs of modern people. When considering ethical questions, a different system of logic is needed, one which recognizes that there is no steady state but accepts constant change. It is a change of paradigm similar to that from Euclidian to Gaussian geometry or from classical to quantum physics. Under the old paradigm, to say that a change was damaging meant that it should be reversed, but under the new, a change back is not necessarily ethical nor even possible. Although, for instance, there is a good case to be made that western nations should never have become involved with Africa, it is not necessarily right to leave its nations alone to wage war against each other with western guns, and struggle with their huge legacy of social problems and economic debt. As another example, every generation of children in western countries receives more help in the form of state subsidies and educational aids than the last; it would not be right to cut these off, though it may well be right to stop increasing this kind of support, much of which has an enfeebling effect.

Clearly a decision as to what is ethical behaviour, which seems simple in the light of our evolutionary history, becomes immensely complicated as a result of our culture.

Examples of the complexity

For instance, conflict may arise between the true interests of those near us, and the way we feel obliged to behave towards them. If someone dependent on me is addicted to smoking, he or she suffers great hardship if I refuse to give him cigarettes, but to do so results in a hazard to his future health.

IMPACT OF TECHNOLOGY ON ETHICAL PRINCIPLES

There may be conflict between natural obligation and wider ethical considerations. If a doctor's wife develops an infection of the lungs, with severe and persistent bronchitis, every time she gets a cold, there is strong pressure on him to treat her colds with antibiotics before the infection develops, even though it may risk the spread of drug resistance.

There is much to be said for the morality of vegetarianism; but if it means forcing one's spouse to do without meat, is it right?

Racial prejudice is a product of cultural advance. Different peoples have moved forward in different places and in different ways, with the result that although we are all very much the same genetically, we have become very different in our appearance and way of life. The perception of those differences causes other groups to become suspicious, and they become xenophobic and define the scapegoats by their obvious features, most commonly their colour. For example, thinking about mixed marriages is confused. It is not the same to say "That person is inferior because he/she is of a different race or nationality" as to say "That person may be an unsuitable mate for my daughter/son because he/she is of a different race or nationality". Mixed marriages do in fact carry risks because of the cultural differences between the parties; it is culture, and not racial origin, that makes people different from each other in habits and attitudes. The risks of a mixed-race marriage are probably mostly removed if the two parties have grown up in the same place or within the same social environment, as happens with people of many races in London and other large cities.

EVOLUTION AND THE NATURE OF GOOD

An example of the class of activity that needs to be continued although it is a step on the way to increased complexity is infection control. Though long ago, as hunter-gatherers, we lived in scattered communities, our increased population later led to our living in more crowded conditions which encouraged infectious diseases, and we responded by finding means to control them, notably hygiene and bactericidal agents. If we now abandoned those methods, the rest of our circumstances remaining unchanged, we, who have lost our immunity because of these measures, would suffer intolerable disease and hardship. Antibiotics, which kill bacteria within the body, have accelerated this process; their immediate effect is for the benefit of individuals rather than the community as a whole, and so they are much in demand in a prosperous democratic society. If they are not taken regularly and the course completed, the few drug-resistant members that every bacterial population contains are able to multiply, causing the emergence of a drug-resistant population. Antibiotics have been the object of much abuse in that they are often used "just in case", or to prevent an infection developing, or to enable a patient to continue work or engage in sports. The result is an increase of the cycle: drug resistance—new agents invented—abuse—new drug resistance.

The movement towards hygiene, which received a great boost in the nineteenth century following the work of Lister, has led to the separation of our lives from those of micro-organisms, whereas previously they were much more interlinked. Children are not allowed to come in contact with anything "dirty", but it is likely that freedom to play on earth and floors was earlier a part of the development of the immune system, giving the child resistance to the same or related infections later. The modern child, not exposed to this informal immunization, continues healthy as long as there is ongoing protection from infection thereafter. A similar mechanism may account for allergies, which have become much more common in recent years. Early in life the body is programmed to accept and recognise many foreign proteins, but if they are withheld and the first exposure occurs at a later stage, it reacts with an attempt to defend against them, in the form of allergy or even anaphylaxis.

After the discovery of disease-bearing micro-organisms in the nineteenth century, all bacteria came to be regarded as the enemy, and every effort was made to kill them whenever an opportunity arose. Only in the latter part of the twentieth century have we come to recognize our partnership with the huge majority of bacteria, notably those in the soil which enable our crops to grow, and those in our intestines which make it possible to digest our food. Even today it is common to see advertisements for bleaches and germicides that "kill all known bacteria".

Driven by the instinct to save life, which was needed for our species' survival in the past, we now save a great many individuals, especially children, who would otherwise have died, and have produced an explosion in the population and many people with long-term disabilities. We could not possibly curb our instinct to preserve lives in this way, but it contributes to the ratchet of development and dependency on our increasingly artificial environment.

EVOLUTION AND THE NATURE OF GOOD

When there was no cure for an illness, no ethical issue arose. Now we have to decide, especially in the case of newborn babies, whether to intervene in ways that will save the baby's life but are likely to result in serious disability. We will always have to live with these decisions—we cannot turn the clock back on existing technology.

We have become unduly preoccupied with sex. Modern conditions cause a distorted attitude towards sex, especially among men. We are almost certainly more concerned about sex than most animals. The reason is that our species has over a relatively short period of archaeological time developed a need for extended child care, strict pairing and control of the sexual instincts. The untrammelled behaviour of many groups of our close relatives the apes—in particular the bonobos—is appropriate for their survival in view of their lifestyle, but humans have been forced into a cultural situation where they have to curb their sexual impulses in the interests of children. In the circumstances of hunter-gatherers, numbers were limited by various factors, as were sexual urges and opportunities, and the small communities meant that everyone knew everyone else, greatly limiting anti-social behaviour. Males were under strong social pressure to limit their sexual encounters. However nowadays the typical family, which until only a few generations ago lived in a settled rural or small-town environment, is caught up in a mêlée of employment, city life and the easy mixing of large numbers of people, in which many sexual opportunities present themselves.

IMPACT OF TECHNOLOGY ON ETHICAL PRINCIPLES

Summary

The aim of this chapter has been to show that the straightforward principles of ethical behaviour derived in the earlier part of this book cannot be simply applied in the presence of advancing culture. Even apes are seen to behave in an anti-social way at times; and the more human societies develop, the more disruption there is of simple moral norms. The maladjustments resulting include the change from a co-operative to a competitive and selfish attitude to our fellows, the politically encouraged meeting of wants rather than needs, and the disruption of family life, which removes much of our ability to give children the care and guidance that they need.

Chapter 10
Key features of ethical behaviour needed in the modern world

Today, to insist on applying the basic principles derived in Chapter 8 would often mean intolerable hardship for oneself or for others. However, we must recognize the same need to help and co-operate with others, and use that paradigm as a guide through the complexities of modern life outlined in Chapter 9. It is impossible to lay down hard-and-fast rules for every situation. Is it right to support an insurrection against political oppression, knowing that it will result for many in death, injury, disablement, bereavement and displacement? Is it ever right to go to war? In all such situations, the individual must consult his/her conscience, bearing in mind the obligation towards other people, and the tapering of such obligation with the genetic and cultural distance from those people.

We need to look at the needs of *Homo*, and see how these can best be met in the altered circumstances of modern life. *Homo*'s needs are considered in *Evolution and the Spiral of Technology*.[1] The original needs of our primordial ancestors were a stable environment, suitable temperature, water, food, fresh air and light. In the course of evolution our forebears acquired a need for companionship and sex, then for care from parents in early

ETHICAL BEHAVIOUR NEEDED IN MODERN WORLD

life; females developed a need to have children. With the acquisition of culture and the ability to migrate and to modify our environment, we came to need clothing and shelter. With the advance of technical skills, the ability to be inactive, which is a feature of all other species, came to be bred out, and we have a need to be constantly creating new things and meeting challenges. Beyond this, we have acquired a need for purpose in our lives, a thread running through our daily activities. Finally, we have a need for needs themselves; if life is too easy and lacking in challenge, it becomes boring and often leads to neurosis of one type or another.

In the modern world we have created an unstable positive feed-back cycle in that by altering our environment to satisfy needs, we create new needs due to the changes, and instead of being reduced, our needs increase.

The common theme in our proper approach to all the problems that have been created in this way is that we have to co-operate and empathize with fellow-beings and indulge our inherited instinct to help them. The "Golden Rule", attributed to Moses, is: consider the interests of others and "love thy neighbour as thyself".[2] An alternative formulation of the commandment is that we do to others as we would have them do to us—this was Darwin's view of ethics.[3] Kant's famous formula was: "Act only on that maxim through which you can at the same time will that it should become a universal law".[4] Jesus' advice was non-reciprocal—charity towards others should be unconditional. The flip side of this charitable attitude, when seen objectively instead of subjectively, is an appreciation that anything which damages ourselves, our families, our lineage and our species, either by harming the biosphere or by making us or our children less suited to the world in which we live, is to be opposed, and anything which helps them is to be encouraged.

Before the cultural explosion of the Holocene (about 10,000 years ago), our species was working towards increasing mutual co-operation, though there were a few practices that we would now find barbaric and unacceptable. It therefore seems right that we should try to restore, as far as possible, the general attitudes that our species had before that explosion took place, and so allow our cycle to proceed to its end in as dignified a manner as it can. The greatest ethical need is to shed the frenetic and materialistic life-style that we have developed during the Holocene.

Care of children

Although the present crisis in family relations and deprivation is largely due to women now abandoning their traditional role, the future should be planned with an acceptance that there is no going back. Since women have come to be educated, motivated and hence professionally ambitious in the same way as men, men should now take on the role of caring for children where it is appropriate. Both parents should be aware of the effects of deprivation on children. In addition to using skills acquired which may make it appropriate for them to go to work, they should decide which parent likes looking after children and is best fitted to do so. Any idea that it is more prestigious to be employed than to care for children should be decisively dropped—biologically the opposite is the case. Ieuan Maddock recommends the re-education of people not to want jobs.[5] We have to regard unemployment as totally respectable, merely one way of residing in the modern state.

"Sex education" is a much debated issue. At the time of writing there has even been much recent discussion about whether children, down to the age of 10-12, should have formal education about homosexuality as an alternative way of life. In the meantime, biology is taught as a remote, objective discipline. It would seem right to teach children about human society and its evolutionary roots, sexual functioning, and family life. These are things which are vital to their happiness and their species' survival, and would be of great interest to them and make biology come much more alive. They would certainly draw their own conclusions and would be in the best position to make decisions as to how to run their lives, without the aid of inhibited neo-Victorians or radical iconoclasts conveying their own particular view of sex.

Woolly thinking about human rights—which are discussed below—together with the rebellion of adolescents against what they see as a false society, has led to confusion about how children should be managed. D.W. Winnicott warns against giving them too much freedom.[6]

EVOLUTION AND THE NATURE OF GOOD

Adjustment of the tax structure

One important measure that our society needs is to make it
again possible for one employee to earn a living for a whole
family. This could conceivably be regulated by a taxation system
which ensures that if both parents are working they get little or no
financial benefit from it. Patricia Morgan's book *Farewell to the
Family*, quoted in a London *Independent* editorial on 15 February
1995, highlights how the British tax system is moving in a
direction to disadvantage couples who stay together, whether
married or not, and have children. Alvin Toffler asks: "Why not
reward, rather than economically punish, those who maintain and
solidify family bonds across generational lines?"[7]

The cult of "liberalism"

The loss of taboos by modern humans has been mentioned in
Chapter 9 in connection with the need of children for family
integrity. In the 20th century we shed our taboos with a
vengeance, and they have become largely an object of ridicule.
Edward Goldsmith writes: "With the breakdown of traditional
societies under the impact of economic development, [taboos]
cease to be operative."[8]

The most important of these taboos are sexual. There is
no easy way to measure how much adultery and casual pre-
marital sex took place in the nineteenth century compared
with the present time. However, the difference is that the
accepted values have changed. To the Victorians, casual

sex was sinful, but now it is allowable and normal behaviour. It no longer seems important to us to remain chaste until we find our life's partner and settle down to raise a family. Bill McKibben writes: "I was born before the sexual revolution and came of age in its wake. Such incredible freedom and creativity is stressful. We want our freedom, in the words of the Cape Cod essayist Robert Finch, 'as children want it and need it—within safe bounds'." [9]

The "media"—newspapers, magazines, television and radio—play a great part in the destruction of taboos. Although freedom of the press is paramount in a democratic country, the media are in reality severely hamstrung by the prevailing fashion in thought. The rights of minorities or of the weak are constantly upheld, and are a popular soap-box for attracting readers. Injustice is great copy. Articles critical of homosexuality, sexual freedom, militantly feminist movements, or African countries' political mismanagement are hard to find, though the occasional exception comes as a breath of fresh air. For instance, an article in the London *Independent* newspaper on 5th July 1993 by Angela Lambert lampoons the extreme fringe of the Women's Lib. movement. She refers to "liberal fascism", and criticises militant feminism, i.e. hatred of men, the demand for an end to family life, and the proposal for artificial insemination and rearing children in all-female communities. "Language", she goes on, "is threatened by the tide of commercially motivated verbal slurry drowning the voice of reason and replacing it with the splutter of the lowest common denominator in pursuit of profit." Political correctness creates a language that has little relation to the way ordinary people express themselves in real life. Again, in April 1994 the British public were treated for an hour on television to a denunciation of "rights" by a cheerful enthusiast. The media also have to promote themselves actively, and so take advantage of the interest that sexual matters arouse in the public. In April 1994 a British television show, in all seriousness, asked viewers to debate the question: "A man discovers that his 20-year-old stepdaughter is in love with him. Should he start a relationship with her?" It was not even specified that he is in love with her too. The public were invited to call in and cast a vote. Although the cynicism of this programme is incredible to any believer in family values, 47% of responses were in favour of the motion, indicating how unimportant these values have become to the British people.

All animal societies observe obligations and taboos.[10] Indeed, taboos, including sexual taboos, are observed slavishly by animals that survive essentially by the maintenance of families, since to break them would have meant extinction. Our culture, by introducing rapid change, restlessness, nuclear families, marital stress, contraception and an intellectual devaluing of taboos, has caused us once again to allow free range to our sexual instincts. Nevertheless, taboos have a vital role in holding our society together, and we ignore them at our peril.

ETHICAL BEHAVIOUR NEEDED IN MODERN WORLD

Rights

The origin of rights

Among animals in general the "law of the jungle" prevails. Prey is chased and caught; each species goes about its daily business in a way modified by evolution to make it safe within reasonable limits. There is no concept of "rights" and no need for one. Among earlier humans a similar state of affairs existed. Communities were small, and within them, the weak took a subordinate position. The "village idiot" type, for instance, was allowed to live on in an inferior role, doing menial work for his superiors in return for sufficient food to survive. Society remained stable, and for its continuance there was no need for human rights. Rights have emerged as a need in modern society where units of population are large, and groups, rather than individuals, develop the power to oppress other groups. As Garrett Hardin says, "Individualistic 'rights' are principally a creation of European civilization; failure to recognize this fact is at the root of many international misunderstandings."[11] The need for rights is seen and acted on by a community when its ruling members see their oppressive practices as endangering their own stability through the threat of revolution.

The French Revolution resulted in the first formal instrument of human rights, the *Déclaration des droits de l'Homme et du Citoyen*, which however addressed neither the status of women nor slavery. Nigel Walker recounts the subsequent history of human rights. They derive from: the political philosophy of

EVOLUTION AND THE NATURE OF GOOD

John Locke, Tom Paine's pamphlet *The Rights of Man*, the Bill of Rights of England and Virginia, the American Declaration of Independence, and the United Nations Declaration of Human Rights. "The parties to the European Convention on Human Rights agreed in 1948 to protect the rights of individuals to life, liberty and security of person ... but adding the important reservation that most of these rights or freedoms could be subject to such restrictions as are prescribed by law and are necessary in a democratic society for certain specified purposes." But the idea of rights, Walker says, is being abused: "... the language of rights is now being used so rhetorically, which means with emotion rather than precision, that some corrective is necessary."[12]

On the rights of offenders, Walker says "We should consider whether instead of talking about 'offenders' rights', a phrase which does not help us to decide whether a right is inalienable, or forfeitable, or curtailable, penologists might find it more helpful to talk about 'discrimination against offenders'."[13]

Walker summarizes as follows: "I have argued that while the concept of 'rights' has been a powerful rhetorical device for the improvement of human conditions, including those of prisoners, it needs a critical examination, even at the risk of being labelled reactionary." Statutes, contracts etc. confer unchallengeable rights; "... but the same cannot be said about 'natural rights', whose status is extremely debatable... The notion of natural rights is thus not on as solid a foundation as it appears. More solid would be a moral principle that there should be no discrimination against categories of people, including offenders, without practical justification, 'practical' being a term which excludes 'retributive' or 'denunciatory'… at least the argument could be based on practicalities rather than faith."[14]

The mis-application of rights

John Barrow and Frank Tipler, in an otherwise ground-breaking 700-page treatise on the very interesting Anthropic Principle, offer a bizarre view of rights, which they believe should be extended to computers: "… the arguments one hears today against considering intelligent computers to be persons and against giving them human rights have precise parallels in the nineteenth-century arguments against giving blacks and women full human rights."[15]

Western *Homo* grossly abuses its rights. Compensation in cash—the modern measure of all rights and wrongs—is being claimed in the courts these days for such things as: being inadequately educated; suffering mental injury in the course of a job in which the type of stress encountered is to be expected; or being scalded in a restaurant by a cup of coffee which was too hot.

In a London *Independent* article on 24 November 1995 entitled *Watch out! There's a victim about*, Polly Toynbee reported that personal injury claims against local authorities had increased eight-fold in 10 years. An atheistical society no longer accepts the concept of the Act of God. "The flip-side of this coin is that some human somewhere is always responsible for everything that happens. There is no more bad luck: someone has to take the blame... Since May, solicitors have been allowed to operate a No Win No Fee service, taking up cases for a 25 per cent share of the proceeds... It makes having a go a very good prospect... There are ambulance-chasing advertising posters up in many accident and emergency departments of hospitals, urging people who have had accidents to contact firms of solicitors... I find it particularly repugnant that people are so eager to sue councils and health authorities for relatively minor matters, thus draining communal funds from the rest of society." Some errors by doctors, like everyone else, are inevitable, but litigation has become an expensive drain on National Health Service resources. "All this is a symptom of an idea of a society in which there is no risk and where no risk is ever acceptable", continues Toynbee. "... it goes far deeper in the national psyche than mere opportunism. It is part of the victim culture, where everyone wants his due with little consideration of what he owes... There used to be a measure of pride and a sense of common ownership in the public services people used. Now people sue them."

On 9 December 1996, an advertisement appeared in the *Independent*, inserted by a group of lawyers who gave a telephone number:

Hurt or injured?
Have you had an accident in the last 3 years?
Was someone else at fault? Find out free
about claiming compensation. Call.

ETHICAL BEHAVIOUR NEEDED IN MODERN WORLD

Hardin believes that "rights" violate the rule that consumption must be kept within sustainable limits. "Much of the rhetoric of 'rights' and 'compassion' is incompatible with rationality. 'Rights' share with 'infinity' the property of limitlessness, which rules out mathematical weighting and calculation, thus ruling out rationality." Rights are often abused because the beneficiaries of them have an opportunity to exceed Hardin's sustainable limits. Thus, for instance, a careless driver injured in an accident may be entitled to medical treatment at public expense, or an unemployed person who does not want to do mean or unattractive work will be kept from penury by the taxpayer. The beneficiary is not accountable; the bill goes to the wrong address.[16]

But probably the most serious abuses of rights are the social ones. In an article by Jonathan Sacks in the *Independent* issue of 6 March 1995 on the damage caused by the decay of the family, he remarked how the idea of rights contributes to its breakdown. "The battle against the family has been conducted in terms of rights—the rights of men to have relationships unencumbered by lasting duties, the rights of women to be free of men, the rights of each of us to plot our private paths to happiness undistracted by the claims of others ...". Proponents of hitherto unaccepted practices, such as homosexuality, will assert their right to influence others, including young people, on the grounds that there is no proof that it does any harm.

In any socialized community individuals are indeed owed rights; but something has gone wrong when individuals are found *insisting* on their rights. We owe rights to others, but when we are in the position of bleating about our own, we have a wrong attitude towards life which will serve us ill and make us unhappy. In the west today we have the unedifying spectacle of people with an inflated standard of living clamouring for their rights, while millions of people in other parts of the world not only have no rights, but are starving or being murdered by the thousand. We have become like this because material gain is the only yardstick we have with which to measure ourselves against each other, and we must be constantly competing with each other for what, except in the artificial context of the technological world, we do not need. Gerd Behrens wrote in *Time* on 25 Oct. 1993: "While collective *duties* reign supreme in the rest of the world, the West celebrates individual *rights*, but that hardly helps the cause of cohesion." (Italics are the present writer's.)

Hardin has some harsh words on the attempt to internationalize rights. "The United Nations Organization", he writes, "has painted the Europeanized world into a corner with its Universal Declaration of Human Rights", which was adopted by the General Assembly in 1948.[17] "Included were such things as the right to a fair trial; freedom of thought, conscience and religion; and the right to work and enjoy social security, education, and the arts." At that time the Assembly was dominated by the western nations. "The drafters of the UN document took no account of a major advance in anthropology and ethnology made at the beginning of the century, namely the idea of ethnocentrism. A moral judgment that is tied to the values of a particular

ETHICAL BEHAVIOUR NEEDED IN MODERN WORLD

group is said to be ethnocentric... The notion of rights that are unique and universal makes for intolerance, whereas sensitivity to the idea of ethnocentrism promotes tolerance...[18] In the nineteenth century Europeans thoughtlessly supported programmes aimed at Christianizing the whole world. In the twentieth century we just as thoughtlessly have demanded a universal devotion to the western version of rights, to which we arrogantly attach the adjective 'universal'. It is very difficult for a Westerner to realize that our version of individualism is only some three centuries old, dating as it does from John Locke (1632-1704). The commitment to 'radical individualism' (as philosophers call it) is confined to a minority of the world's five billion people."[19] It is likely that the indecent speed with which the Eastern European communist regimes were replaced after 1989 by hastily-assembled democracies, throwing the countries into economic chaos and many of the people into unemployment and poverty, owed much to western pressure for human rights. Harold Dickinson pointed out that the People's Republic of China, established in 1949, introduced a system of 78,000 People's Communes ranging in size from 6,000 to 60,000 people, which reversed the drift of population from the land to the cities. At that time China had 760 million people, and 80% of them worked on the land or in related activities. The people lived simply, and their main occupation was growing food. Dickinson "writes that the mass of the rural population accepts the rule of the Communist Party, which has greatly

EVOLUTION AND THE NATURE OF GOOD

reduced the possibility of widespread flood or famine, and has provided adequate food, housing, and basic social services. He sees the emphasis on the use of local materials in intensive agriculture as an important lesson in development."[20] Should western nations work to overthrow this system, without regard to the consequences to the Chinese people, in the interests of what they consider as human rights?

Mary Warnock makes a "central point" about rights and duties. "If someone claims a legal right, then this entails that someone has a duty to see that the right is respected." But when it comes to fundamental human rights, "it is mere rhetoric to try to extend these rights beyond a few that would be agreed to be basic... I deplore the thoughtless issuing, towards the end of the twentieth century, of so-called charters, the parents' charter, the rail-users' charter, the patients' charter... There cannot be a morality founded on the concept of rights."[21]

Real rights

John Finnis lists what he regards as absolute human rights: (1) the right not to have one's life taken; (2) The right not to be positively lied to; (3) The right not to be condemned on knowingly false charges; (4) The right not to be deprived of one's procreative capacity; and (5) The right to be taken into respectful consideration in any assessment of what the common good requires.[22]

ETHICAL BEHAVIOUR NEEDED IN MODERN WORLD

Equality and "equal rights"

Warnock makes a very important distinction between *equality* and *equal rights*. The former recognizes the equal importance of all humans, while the latter "imposes" rights on individuals which may be inappropriate or even harmful.[23] Examples are children, mental patients, and women and others in societies which depend for their welfare and stability on a dominance hierarchy. Mental patients at some, probably most, British units have no restrictions made on their right to smoke too much, to eat too much, to refuse to do any work and to lounge about all day. They have the same freedom to buy street drugs as any other person. Behind all this potentially damaging permissiveness there is almost certainly a fear felt by the authorities of being accused of violating their patients' rights.

Rights vary with time and circumstance

The view of "rights" is constantly changing. Early in the 20th century the rights of women in Britain were recognized, but those of blacks not until the middle of the century. Western rulers now pay much attention to disadvantaged groups, who can exert considerable pressure through the media and the vote. The rights thus identified are conferred by the community as a whole, not as conceived by a minority on their own behalf; they are conferred because it has become expedient for the majority.

Warnock argues that if a right which is claimed has not been specifically conferred or accrued as a result of a contract, it cannot be claimed as an absolute right, for all humans and for all time, since it may well be a right intended to apply only at a specific time, in specific circumstances and for some people, not others. She quotes as an example the very didactic wording of the 1990 UNICEF charter of children's rights, which does not make provision for the decisions that have to be made about ailing newborn babies.[24]

The conflict between rights and society's needs

Human rights often conflict with the general interest, as in the case of the psychiatric patient allowed out on parole who commits more murders or rapes. The problem of alleged child abusers (injustice to people refused work in child care because of suspicion) illustrates how natural law and equity conflicts with human justice. To protect children, society has to be unjust to the suspects.

Perception of rights is subjective

John Finnis points out that rights cannot be conferred by calculation in a utilitarian manner. "Rather, such judgements are arrived at by a steady determination to respect human good in one's own existence and the equivalent humanity or human rights of others ... rather than trade off that good and those rights against some vision of future 'net best consequences', consequences which overall, both logically and practically, one cannot know, cannot control or dispose of, and cannot evaluate."[25]

For Warnock, public morality, in the form of law and justice, confers rights, but private morality "is necessarily concerned with individuals, their motives, characters and consciences." It is based on the possibility of self-denial or altruism. "It is my contention that a civil society could not function if it subsisted only on indignation where rights had been infringed ..."[26]

Rights and obligations

Rights can best be seen subjectively as *obligations* to others. When it is held that people have *rights*, it is not stated whose duty it is to fill those rights; but when it is held that people have *obligations*, it is clear on whom the obligation rests. It is therefore more practical, and leads to less confusion and ambiguity, to define obligations that people owe rather than rights.

Animal rights

The term "human rights" implies that humans have rights that other animals do not have. Yet there is no absolute sense in which that is true; it is a viewpoint held only by humans. (To Richard Dawkins, human rights, human dignity, and the sacredness of human life are forms of "speciesism".[27]) It can, however, be said that *Homo* is the only species that has acquired a need for rights to protect its individuals from their own species.

Like human rights, animal rights are very relative; our conception of them varies with our genetic distance from the animal concerned and the degree to which we are inter-dependent with it. It is more realistic to stress the *avoidance of cruelty* to animals.

Blame and punishment

The lesson of biology and evolution is that people do things because they are impelled by external forces. It follows that our society does the unthinkable, i.e. punishes people for things that are no fault of their own. Yet punishment is necessary in modern society, in order to prevent the recurrence of the anti-social act punished. With socialization and the advance of human culture, we now have the right to trial, in the course of which the judge and jury seek the cause of the deed and may decide it is not the defendant's fault. The emphasis has partly changed, from preventing anti-social behaviour to being fair to the accused.

In this way we have formalized punishment, whereas animals and primitive societies have reacted directly to the violation by killing or striking the offender, without formulating the intermediate "truth" that what they did was wrong, or against the law, etc. Unlike these societies, modern humans, with their obsession for "truth", must allocate blame, must say "He/she has sinned" before inflicting the punishment. Thus, in July

ETHICAL BEHAVIOUR NEEDED IN MODERN WORLD

1993 a British judge said: "You are an evil person, deserving of the four life sentences I am imposing on you." The judge was taking an absolute view of good and evil. Although people, as seen from outside, behave according to cause-and-effect rules, blame is laid on them and they are punished according to their "deserts"—this is the yardstick—rather than according to the needs of society.   Legal decisions may also be made in order to exact revenge on a wrongdoer by the community or by a bereaved relative. Winnicott, commenting on the *Report of the Committee on Punishment in Prisons and Borstals* in 1961, wrote: "It is impossible to get away from the principle that the first function of the law is to express the unconscious revenge of society... we cannot think only in terms of treating individual criminals, forgetting that society has been wounded and also needs treatment."[28] Formal recognition is given to two theories of punishment: the retributive theory (punishment according to deserts) and the utilitarian theory (based on the consequences of the punishment, which include that the subject be reformed and that other people be deterred from crime).[29]

Blame vs expediency

Once it is accepted that biology, cause and effect, is the driving force in humans it becomes incorrect to speak in terms of blame. More and more, society is recognizing that people's behaviour is caused. A paedophile, for instance, is not so by choice; he does not act as he does because he thinks he will be better off because of it; he is impelled. Is it right to label his behaviour as illness or sin? Sin means something you could do but could avoid doing. In many cases the authorities are exercised whether to commit a social offender to prison or to a mental institution. In the former case it is because he/she is at fault, to blame, and in the latter case it is because he is afflicted with an illness, for which he is not to blame.

The outcome of all this is that we need a new way of thinking about why we take various measures when people commit social violations. The object is to protect society, and since we recognize the caused nature of human behaviour, the effect is necessarily to penalise people who commit these offences, regardless of whether it is their "fault" or not. To be realistic, we have to punish some people for the reason that they are a menace to society, without reference to the question of blame.

What then should be the yardstick to decide who should go to prison and who to a mental institution? It would seem that if the punishment is expected to result in better behaviour by the person involved, or by other people, legal measures are appropriate. If not, the deviant should presumably be handled and/or confined in such a way as to prevent him/her from repeating the crime, in the most comfortable way possible. This may include permanent incarceration for the rest of life. Clearly mental patients, who cannot be regarded as to blame, may sometimes have to be permanently confined. "When the detention is no longer justifiable as retribution, denunciation, deterrence or correction, but solely as a protection for others", writes Walker, "its conditions should be no worse, apart from the deprivation of liberty, than those which a law-abiding wage-

ETHICAL BEHAVIOUR NEEDED IN MODERN WORLD

earner would enjoy outside."[30]   Seen this way, the idea of "blame" should be entirely restricted to those who are expected to do better after being punished, or whose punishment will serve as an example to others.

Walker discusses the issue of incarceration to protect the public. "What has made the concept of dangerousness a really live issue is the shortening of the periods of detention which legislators, sentencers and psychiatrists regard as justified on other grounds. Why shouldn't the protection of the public be regarded as justification which is quite as sound as retribution, deterrence or the need for treatment? There is an answer which is based, fundamentally, on the argument that you may have a right to detain someone for something which he *has* done, or at least attempted or risked by his recklessness or negligence, but not for something which he has *not done* but might do.[31] ... the general principle, I suggest, must be that the need to detain any involuntary patient beyond six months should be reviewed at regular intervals by some authoritative body of people who are all completely independent of the hospital in which the patient is detained." Because of solidarity between psychiatrists, " ... the decision should be by a confidential vote, so that his colleagues need not know whether he voted for or against it; and there should always be enough non-psychiatrists to outvote the psychiatrists." Prosecution should always be done if a mentally disordered patient commits a crime; but this does not solve the problem of the patient who has not actually done or attempted anything that could have resulted in serious harm, but has merely talked about doing it.   To dispose of someone by

EVOLUTION AND THE NATURE OF GOOD

custody, however liberally managed, "is to deprive him of much that makes life worth living. Almost any degree of non-custodial control is preferable."[32]

It is worth noting that in primitive communities such people as child abusers and violent psychopaths would simply have been destroyed on the spot. In the course of change to modern ways of handling offenders, the use of capital punishment has only gradually left our society, recently, as nations have become wealthier and able to house and control more prisoners, and as social conscience has increased at the same time.

Vengeance still plays its part in the law; but it is compassion that now has the greatest influence in separating legal decisions from crime prevention. A schizophrenic murderer may escape being institutionalized for life because it is not his fault, a rapist may be released after a period for good behaviour, or a felon who is a mother is left at large because her children need her. We cannot retreat from this compassionate position, but it detracts from the efficiency of crime prevention. The attempt to retreat further and further from punitive measures, in the name of humanity, for those who have been deemed not responsible for their actions, puts society more and more at risk from offenders. Raymond M. Smullyan, in an article entitled "Is God a Taoist?", underlines the illogicality of the legal view in a conversation between God and a mortal. God says: "At last you see the point ... that sinning is not the real issue! The important thing is that people as well as other sentient beings don't get hurt!"[33]

ETHICAL BEHAVIOUR NEEDED IN MODERN WORLD

We are in the embarrassing position that while we have to act against anti-social behaviour to prevent its recurrence, we can also determine its causes by scientific means. It is against the interests of the community to allow these causes to be advanced as a defence. That line of reasoning might make criminals claim it is the determinism of our animal nature that causes their activities, and that therefore they should not be punished.[34] Melvin Konner writes: "I feel a great impatience with social scientists (or for that matter, lawyers) who try to explain away acts of selfishness or brutality by reference to psychological facts and principles... The law is not an instrument of explanation, it is an instrument of justice, of protection, of redress of grievances, and of punishment of wrongdoing... The law should judge, but the scientist should still explain, irrespective of what the law may do."[35] As increasing thought and research are devoted to the causes of crime, inevitably a reason will be found for more and more crimes, driving the authorities into the corner where they can cannot mete out punishment because it is not deserved. The ultimate outcome of such research, if it could be completed, would be that all crime, like all action by humans and other living things, is the result of previous causes and not due to the volition of the committer.

As with our animal ancestors, our way to survival is by preventing actions that disrupt our society. To that end, those that fall foul of the system have to be punished, without regard to the cause of the misdeed—which is pre-determined whether the felon is a raving lunatic or an apparently normal member of the community. The punishment needs to be publicized, to deter others as well as the offender. If it is accepted that all responses to a given situation are caused by extraneous factors—inherited or developmental—then there is no greater injustice in incarcerating someone whose actions are clearly the result of severe deprivation or abuse in childhood, than in doing this when the reason for the behaviour is not easily discoverable. Perhaps this unfairness was what was in the mind of Jesus when he summed up the parable of the talents with these not-very-Christian-sounding words: "Unto every one that hath shall be given, and he shall have abundance; but from him that hath not shall be taken away even that which he hath." (Matthew 25,29).

When a human community inflicts punishment, it is saying to the one convicted "You are unfortunate enough to be incompatible with us, the mainstream of society, so we reject and fine, incarcerate, or kill you [as the case may be]." We should recognize that this is what we are doing, so as to apply justice in the most realistic, efficient, and humane way possible.

A rational thinker can blame him/herself but not others

If the world is deterministic, and all its events are caused by previous events, there is no sense in attributing "blame" to anyone for violating proper behaviour. When it comes to oneself, however, the laws of the physical world do not apply. As I have discussed in *Evolution and the Nature of Reality*, the subjective is the origin of reality, and the physical world is derived from it.[36] To myself, subjectively, I *do* have free-will, even if from outside my actions seem to be caused. For this reason it is both possible and right for me to blame myself for bad behaviour, and to try and do better next time. Such a process of thought can certainly be reviewed by an outside scientist, and seen as a logical cause-and-effect process which is the result of my involved membership of the human race and my obligation to my fellows. As it presents itself to *me*, however, I have to blame myself for my lapses and make an effort to improve. To A C Ewing, "Practically it is perhaps a good dictum for most purposes that we should adopt the indeterminist attitude towards ourselves and the determinist attitude towards other men, in the sense that we should think of ourselves as capable of going against all the causes by which the psychologist would explain our conduct but prepared always to look for the causes to explain the unsatisfactory conduct of other men."[37]

Ethics changes with time

For an understanding of a person's concept of what is right, one has to look at the time when it was held (as well as the place), and the nature of the community in which it was held. Moral standards have to change continually with the "progress" of mankind.[38] A Christian ethic that was valid in the time of Christ may be different now, with the emancipation of women and other social changes. Huckleberry Finn's dilemma, referred to in Chapter 9, is a good example. Others from Southern Africa's long history of race relations may be considered. Olive Schreiner, the 19th century South African liberal writer, referred to the black people in her book *The Story of an African Farm* as

EVOLUTION AND THE NATURE OF GOOD

"kaffirs", and discussed them as if they were naturally a servant class.[39]   Cecil Rhodes, to the British of his time, was a great empire builder and a hero, but today he is seen as an ambitious, grasping, self-interested imperialist.   Garfield Todd's appointment as Prime Minister of Southern Rhodesia in 1953 was a remarkable achievement, in view of his liberalism and the reactionary attitude of the white electorate.   His United Rhodesian party later removed him from the leadership because of his liberal stance, and after Ian Smith's declaration of independence from Britain in 1965 he was restricted by Smith's government. Yet he was severely criticised in an obituary by a British journalist in 1992 for his failure to produce positive African advancement, and for saying that to hand over power to the majority at that time would be disastrous.

Ethics is thus a very subjective study; although the principles are constant, good behaviour judged in retrospect and in various environments depends on its circumstances. Is there some way we can judge the behaviour of people objectively no matter at what time they lived? Perhaps the key pointer is the *attitude* of an individual towards others in the context of the society in which she/he lives.   There are tales of kind guards in Nazi concentration camps; Nelson Mandela formed a lasting friendship with one of his Robben Island warders. We can't all be heroes, yet it is a commonly-held assumption that all those in certain evilly-directed groups who are not social reformers are in the wrong. The absolute in all this can be seen as the extent to which we relate to others. In relating, we recognize the quality of all humans. The exercise of sympathy and empathy is the good, antagonism and rejection the bad.

How should we respond to the challenge posed by the advance of technology?

In my book *Evolution and the Spiral of Technology* it is concluded that the inroads made by technology are causing ever-increasing stress and leading towards social collapse. In that book, the extent to which we have become dependent on changes already wrought in our environment are classified:

(a) Changes on which we have become so dependent that to reverse them would cause intolerable hardship. To do so would be wrong.

(b) Those which it would be an effort to reverse, but it could be done. Here it would need fine judgment to decide on the correct response.

(c) Those which it would be in our individual interests to reverse, as well as in the interests of humankind and the biosphere as a whole, such as by eating more wholesome food, or taking regular exercise. The right thing is to do away with the harmful changes. As regards these matters of personal health, one should reduce ones dependency on others and on the social services, so it is an ethical issue and not merely a matter of self-interest.

(d) Those which have not yet taken place, though there is constant pressure for change.[40]

EVOLUTION AND THE NATURE OF GOOD

Certain general guidelines can be suggested, based on the facts that the oldest cultural practices are the most deeply entrenched, the most recently developed ones are in general the most harmful, and those that have not yet been adopted need not happen at all. On this basis, the first priority is to avoid taking measures which will complicate our lives further and accelerate the technology spiral, for instance the invention and use of faster cars and more efficient computers, developing nuclear power, and installing a lift when the stairs would do. There is no biological, sociological or ethical justification for such changes, although their daily occurrence is accepted and taken for granted by everybody. The second priority is to drop recently-adopted practices and habits which are damaging to individuals and to society, but which at the same time have not become an essential part of life. High among these are activities harmful to health, including overeating, particularly of sophisticated fatty, high-calorie, low-fibre foods, and the use of cars and buses instead of walking or cycling. When cultural needs have become entrenched it may sometimes be regarded as ethical to fulfil them, even though this may contribute to the acceleration of the human cycle and the earlier collapse of our society. The complexity of such ethical choices in the modern world is increased by the difficulty of deciding which practices are entrenched and which can be abandoned without causing unacceptable distress.

ETHICAL BEHAVIOUR NEEDED IN MODERN WORLD

Summary

A thread runs through the various topics discussed in this chapter. To behave ethically in any situation we have to be charitable, to give reign to our instinct for empathy and fellowship with others, whether they be children, lovers, life partners, relatives, fellow humans or living things other than humans. Often such behaviour demands a measure of sacrifice, sometimes severe; that is the price we pay for our advanced culture. Consideration for others underpins the trouble, time and commitment needed for the care of children, the thoughtfulness and forbearance required for a tranquil and sustainable married life, and the respect due to a lover and possible future life partner and future children. It stops one from becoming a burden, practical or emotional, on those with whom one lives. It causes one to hold and express responsible opinions, rather than support causes because they are popular or get one elected. Charity makes us see how external forces affect other people's behaviour, and sympathize with the many problems that our fellow-humans inevitably endure in the modern world, rather than apportion blame. The same attitude, applied in a global way to the whole of humanity and to the biosphere as a whole, makes one think deeply about the damage that our technological advancement is doing to the environment, and the multiplying human problems and stresses that result.

REFERENCES

Introduction
1. Darwin (1871) 165   2. Murdoch 68   3. Shennan (2003) 90-2   4. Murdoch 96
5. Singer (1994) 58   6. Foot 67   7. Ibid. 75,79   8. Singer 58   9. Quinton 20.

Chapter 1
1. Shennan (2003)   2. Wilson 165-6   3. Ewing 115-43 & 180-1   4. Edwards & Pap 29
5. Midgley 33   6. Edwards and Pap 294   7. Ridley 50 seq.   8. Skolimowski 80
9. Gould (1991) 401   10. Watson 936   11. Steiner 236   12. Jacob 425
13. Wilson 96   14. Polanyi 195   15. Jacob 363-4   16. Konner 422   17. Gjertsen 143-4
18. Ibid. 67   19. Schrödinger (1958) 137-8   20. Heisenberg 190   21. Mencius 28
22. Midgley 3,136   23. Murdoch   24. Shennan (2003) 104-7   25. Warnock 137
26. Ibid. 149-53.

Chapter 2
1. Armstrong 10   2. Ibid. 24   3. Ibid. 22   4. Shennan (2003) 72-97   5. Armstrong 347,442
6. Ibid. 67-9   7. Ibid. 39-40   8. Ibid.45-6   9. Singer (1994) 180.   10. Watson 262
11. Ibid. 422-4   12. Ibid. 265   13. Holloway   14. Armstrong 82-5   15. Ibid. 201-2   16. Ibid. 136
17. Ibid. 360-5   18. Ibid. 366   19. Watson 1008   20. Ibid. 1010   21. Shennan (2003) 62.

Chapter 3
1. Singer (1994) 179   2. Ibid. 203   3. Ibid 189   4. Clay 461   5.Huxley   6. Singer (1994) 181
7. Ibid. 279   8. Warnock 119   9. Singer (2001) 9   10. Singer (1994) 161   11. Ibid. 113-6
12. Ibid. 219-20   13. Ewing 44   14. Singer (1994) 204   15. Ibid. 314   16. Jacob (1982) 376-8
17. Gould (1983) 32-45   18. Thompson (1994) 136   19. Ewing 98   20. Thompson (1994) 213-4
21. Ibid. 56   22. Winston 178   23. Gould (1983) 42   24. Gould (1991) 327
25. Schrödinger (1958) 99-101   26. Wilson 196   27. Toffler 410   28. Boyden 96
29. Gould (1983) 44   30. Gould (1991) 327   31. Wilson 5   32. Midgley 159
33. Thompson (1995) 137   34. Thompson (1994) 70   35. Darwin 70-106   36. Midgley
37. Katz   38. Gould (1991) 336   39. Rosenberg 138   40. Ridley 144   41. Ibid. 38
42. Shennan (2003) 62-3   43. Warnock 111   44. Rachels 90,129-30   45. Ibid. 1   46. Ibid. 97
47. Ibid. 171   48. Ibid. 196-7   49. Foot 56   50. Singer (1994) 6.

Chapter 4
1. Gribbin 235-6   2. Sagan and Druyan 298   3. Ibid. 302   4. Devall 123   5. Capra 17-22
6. Konner 298-300   7. Sagan and Druyan 299   8. Gribbin 241-2   9. Winnicott 101   10. Bowlby
11. Ibid. 8   12. Ibid. 11-2   13. Ibid. 13   14. Ibid. 16-7   15. Ibid. 16-29   16. Ibid. 35   17. Ibid. 62
18. Ibid. 62   19. Sagan and Druyan 354   20. Konner 313   21. Bowlby 75-6
22. Winnicott 103   23. Bowlby 78   24. Ibid. 77   25. Ibid. 181   26. Wilson 134
27. Winnicott 111   28. Morris 94   29. Ibid. 106   30. Ibid. 109-10   31. Konner 243-244
32. Schrödinger (1992) 177   33. Konner 302-4   34. Ibid. 309   35. Ibid. 307   36. Wilson 125   37.
Gribbin 228   38. Sagan and Druyan 329   39. Gribbin 228   40. Marais 200-3
41. Konner 267   42. Diamond 7-78   43. Konner 315   44. Ibid. 316   45. Diamond 56-9
46. Singer (1994) 60-1   47. Midgley 146   48. Singer (1994) 57   49. Midgley 182
50. Wilson 149-53   51. Ibid. 156-7   52. Ibid. 157   53. Wright 182-4   54. Diamond 37.

Chapter 5
1. Hayden 158   2. Katz 4   3. Ibid. 8   4. Shennan (2000) 123   5. Sagan and Druyan 347
6. Ibid. 406   7. Ibid. 367-8   8. Konner 35   9. Ibid. 40   10. Ibid. 34   11. Singer (1994) 35-6
12. Wright 378   13. Singer (2001) 244   14. Ibid. 248   15. Ibid. 279   16. Shennan (2000) 129-32
17. Sagan and Druyan 300   18. Katz 10-5   19. Singer (1994) 34   20. Ardrey 329-30
21. Cohen 19-20   22. Hardin 176-7   23. Shennan (2003) 72-97   24. Ardrey
25. Shennan (2000) 115-8   26. Stringer and McKie 64   27. Diamond 46
28. Stringer and McKie 112-4   29. Harth 36-8   30. Diamond 43-4   31. Kingdon 303
32. Stringer and McKie 173   33. Ibid. 181   34. Ibid. 170   35. Singer (1994) 34   36. Ibid.37-8
37. Ibid. 157.

Chapter 6
1. Singer (1994) 362-5   2. Ibid. 378-9   3. Ibid.   4. Ardrey   5. Warnock 127   6. Singer (1994) 11
7. Hardin 235   8. Ibid. 306   9. Singer (1994) 381   10. Singer (2001) 29   11. Ibid. 101
12. Singer (1994) 61-2   13. Rachels 155   14. Ewing 77   15. Shennan (2000) 59-65
16. Hardin 177.

Chapter 7
1. Singer (1994) 5   2. Ibid. 59   3. Winston 301   4. Flew 47   5. Gribbin 213   6. Murdoch 37
7. Ibid. 33   8. Midgley 3   9. Rachels 147   10. Ibid. 149   11. Midgley 119   12. Ibid. 131
13. Sagan and Druyan 315   14. Midgley 173   15. Hayden 154-8   16. Shennan (2000) 187-94
17. Shennan (2003) 62-4   18. Singer (1994) 169.

Chapter 8
1. Wright 139-41   2. Bowlby 11-2   3. Wright 125   4. Bowlby   5. Wright 139   6. Ibid. 133-7
7. Diamond 51   8. Toffler 228   9. Midgley 146.

Chapter 9
1. Hayden 361   2. Ibid.149   3. Ibid. 439   4. Ibid. 197   5. Ibid. 200-8   6. Ibid. 210-1
7. Ibid. 225   8. Ibid. 244   9. Ibid. 250   10. Ibid. 268   11. Ibid. 292   12. Ibid. 310   13. Ibid. 268
14. Ibid. 306   15. Ibid. 347   16. Ibid.355   17. Ibid.358   18. Ibid. 359   19. Ibid. 366
20. Ibid 403   21. Ibid. 387   22. Ibid. 391   23. Singer (1994) 294-305   24. Watson 763-4
25. Cohen 29   26. Sagan & Druyan 406   27. Diamond 265-6   28. Wright 219   29. Illich 10 seq.
30. Hayden 269   31. Capra 202   32. Ibid. 218-23   33. Ibid. 230   34. Ibid. 234   35. Ibid. 241   36.
Coyle   37. Singer (2001) 57-65   38. Rivers 45   39. Sacks   40. Ibid.23-30   41. Toffler 42
42. Ardrey 149   43. Bowlby 82-3   44. Ardrey 149   45. Gribbin 229   46. Bowlby 84
47. Ibid. 105   48. Toffler 221   49. Wilson 135-7   50. Miringoff 75,87,111   51.Konner 245
52. Sagan & Druyan 291   53. Diamond 93   54. Gribbin 231-2   55. Kingdon 316.

Chapter 10
1. Shennan (2000) 159-66   2. Singer (2001) 14   3. Darwin 165   4. Singer (2001) 14
5. Maddock 592-4   6. Winnicott 209-19   7. Toffler 379-80   8. Goldsmith 257   9. McKibben 93
10. Ardrey 361-2   11. Hardin 232   12. Walker 165   13. Ibid. 182   14. Ibid. 187-8
15. Barrow and Tipler 595   16. Hardin 245-6   17. Ibid. 268   18. Ibid. 295-6   19. Ibid. 269-70
20. Rivers 143-5   21. Warnock 100-1   22. Singer (1994) 257-8   23. Warnock 21   24. Ibid. 93-4
25. Singer (1994) 258   26. Warnock 106-7   27. Dawkins 114   28. Winnicott 202-3
29. Ewing 166-8   30. Walker 104   31. Ibid. 93-4   32. Ibid. 110-2
33. Hofstadter and Dennett 327-8   34. Sagan and Druyan 405   35. Konner 179-80
36. Shennan (2003) 33-6   37. Ewing 164   38. Holloway 148-9   39. Schreiner
40. Shennan (2000) 204-5.

BIBLIOGRAPHY

Ardrey, Robert (1970). The Social Contract. London: Fontana.

Armstrong, Karen (1993) A History of God. London: Vintage 1999.

Barrow, John D. and Tipler, Frank J. (1986) The Anthropic Cosmological Principle. Oxford: OUP 1988.

Bowlby, John (1953) Child Care and the Growth of Love. London: Pelican.

Boyden, Stephen (1992) The human aptitude for culture & its biological consequences. Perspectives in Human Biology, No.1.

Capra, Fritjof (1982) The Turning Point. London: Flamingo 1983.

Charon, Jean (Ed.) (1987) The Real and the Imaginary: a new approach to physics. New York: Paragon House.

Clay, Henry (1942) Economics for the General Reader. London: MacMillan.

Cohen, Mark Nathan (1989) Health and the Rise of Civilization. New Haven: Yale University Press.

Coyle, Diana (2007) The Soulful Science. Oxford: Princeton University Press.

Darwin, Charles (1871) The Descent of Man, & Selection in Relation to Sex. Princeton: Princeton UP, 1981.

Dawkins, Richard (1986) The Blind Watchmaker. London: Penguin 1991.

Devall, Bill (1988) Simple in Means, Rich in Ends: practising deep ecology. London: Green Print 1990.

Diamond, Jared (1991) The Rise and Fall of the Third Chimpanzee. London: Vintage.

Dixon, Bernard (Ed.) (1989) From Creation to Chaos: classic writings in science. London: Cardinal 1991.

Edwards, Paul and Pap, Arthur (1973) A Modern Introduction to Philosophy. New York: Free Press.

Ewing, A.C. (1953) Teach Yourself Ethics. London: English Universities Press.

Flew, Anthony (1967) Evolutionary Ethics. London: Macmillan.

Foot, Philippa (2001) Natural Goodness. New York: Oxford University Press.

Gjertsen, Derek (1989) Science and Philosophy, past and present. London: Penguin 1992.

Goldsmith, Edward (1992) The Way: an ecological world-view. London: Rider.

Gould, Stephen Jay (1983) Hen's Teeth and Horse's Toes. London: Penguin 1990.

Gould, Stephen Jay (1991) Bully for Brontosaurus. London: Penguin 1992.

Gribbin, Mary and Gribbin, John (1993) Being Human; putting people in an evolutionary perspective. London: Dent.

Hardin, Garrett (1993) Living Within Limits: ecology, economics & population taboos. Oxford: OUP.

Harth, Erich (1990) Dawn of a Millenium: beyond evolution and culture. London: Penguin 1971.

Hayden, Brian (1993) Archaeology – the science of once and future things. New York: W H Freeman.

Heisenberg, Werner (1962) Physics and Philosophy: the revolution in modern science. London: Pelican 1989.

Hofstadter, Douglas R. and Dennett, Daniel C. (1981) The Mind's I. London: Penguin 1982.

Holloway, Richard (1999) Godless Morality. Edinburgh: Canongate.

Huxley, Aldous (1932) Brave New World. London: Folio Society 1997.

Illich, Ivan (1973) Tools for Conviviality. London: Calder and Boyars.

Jacob, François (1982) The Possible and the Actual. London: Penguin 1989.

Katz, Leonard D. (2000) Evolutionary Origins of Morality. Exeter: Imprint Academic.
Kingdon, Jonathan (1993) Self-made Man and his Undoing. London: Simon and Schuster.
Konner, Melvin (1984) The Tangled Wing: biological constraints on the human spirit. London: Penguin 1993.
Lewin, Roger (1993) Complexity: life at the edge of chaos. London: Phoenix 1993.
Maddock, Ieuan (1978) Beyond the Protestant Ethic. New Scientist Vol. 80, No. 1130, Nov. 23.
Marais, Eugene (1969) The Soul of the Ape. Cape Town: Human and Rousseau.
McKibben, Bill (1990) The End of Nature. London: Penguin 1990.
Mencius, (c.350 B.C.) Are Humans Good by Nature? In Singer, Peter (see ref. below).
Midgley, Mary (1994) The Ethical Primate. London: Routledge.
Miringoff, Marc L.(1999) The Social Health of the Nation. New York/Oxford: OUP.
Morris, Desmond (1967) The Naked Ape. London: Corgi 1968.
Murdoch, Iris (1970) The Sovereignty of Good. London: Routledge.
Polanyi, Michael (1958) An extract from *Personal Knowledge*. In Dixon, Bernard (see ref. above).
Quinton, Anthony (1973) Utilitarian Ethics. London: MacMillan.
Rachels, James (1990) Created from Animals. Oxford: Oxford University Press.
Ridley, Matt (1996) The Origins of Virtue. London: Penguin 1997.
Rivers, Patrick (1975) The Survivalists. London: Eyre Methuen.
Rosenberg, Alexander (2000) Darwinism in Philosophy, Social Science and Policy. Cambridge: Cambridge University Press.
Sacks, Jonathan (1995) Faith in the Future. London: Darton, Longman and Todd.
Sagan, Carl & Druyan, Ann (1992) Shadows of Forgotten Ancestors: a search for who we are. London: Century.
Schreiner, Olive (1883) The Story of an African Farm. London: Penguin 1971.
Schrödinger, Erwin (1958) Mind and Matter. Cambridge: Cambridge University Press 1992.
Schrödinger, Erwin (1992) Autobiographical Sketches. Cambridge: Cambridge University Press.
Shennan, D. H. (2000) Evolution and the Spiral of Technology. Victoria, B.C.: Trafford.
Shennan, D.H (2003) Evolution and the Nature of Reality. Victoria, B.C.: Trafford.
Singer, Peter (1994) Ethics. Oxford: Oxford University Press.
Singer, Peter (2001). Writings on an Ethical Life. London: Fourth Estate.
Skolimowski, Henryk (1987) The Interactive Mind in the Participatory Universe. In Charon, Jean (see ref. above).
Steiner, George (1978) Has Truth a Future? Bronowski Memorial Lecture. In Dixon, Bernard (see ref. above).
Stringer, Chris and McKie, Robin (1996) African Exodus: the origins of modern humanity. London: Jonathan Cape.
Thompson, Mel (1994) Teach Yourself Ethics. London: Hodder Headline.
Thompson, Mel (1995) Teach Yourself Philosophy. London: Hodder Headline.
Toffler, Alvin (1980) The Third Wave. London: Pan 1981.
Walker, Nigel (1980) Punishment, Danger & Stigma. Oxford: Basil Blackwell.
Warnock, Mary (1998) An Intelligent Person's Guide to Ethics. London: Duckbacks 2001.
Watson, Peter (2005) Ideas: A History from Fire to Freud. London: Phoenix 2006.
Wilson, Edward O. (1978) On Human Nature. Cambridge, Mass.: Harvard University Press.
Winnicott, D.W. (1984) Deprivation and Delinquency. Routledge 1990.
Winston, Robert (2002) Human Instinct. London: Bantam Press.
Wright, Robert (1994) The Moral Animal. London: Abacus 1996.

INDEX

INDEX

EVOLUTION AND THE NATURE OF GOOD

INDEX

EVOLUTION AND THE NATURE OF GOOD

INDEX